ALFRE BASIC ADULT THEORY PIANO BOOK

LEVEL THREE

WILLARD A. PALMER MORTON MANUS AMANDA VICK LETHCO

FOREWORD

This Theory Book may be assigned when the student begins Alfred's Adult Lesson Book Three.

In this book all the scales and keys previously introduced are reviewed, and the following new scales and keys are explored in depth, including the primary chords of each key, in all positions: A MAJOR, F♯ MINOR, E MAJOR, C♯ MINOR, E♭ MAJOR, C MINOR, AND A♭ MAJOR.

The study of the keys around the CIRCLE OF FIFTHS is continued and completed.

The DIMINISHED CHORD is reviewed, with emphasis on the proper spelling of the chord.

Alberti bass is also reviewed and emphasized.

From the beginning of this book, the student is introduced to the names of all the degrees of the scale. This is very important information that should be known by every student. It helps greatly with the understanding of chord progressions, transposition, and many other aspects of music.

At the end of this book, the most frequently used ornaments are thoroughly reviewed.

Assign with the beginning of ADULT LESSON Book 3.

Scale Degrees: Tonic, Dominant, Subdominant

The tones of a scale are also called the *degrees* of the scale. Each *scale degree* has a name.

- The KEY-NOTE (the tone of the same name as the scale) is called the **TONIC.**
- The tone a 5th ABOVE the tonic is called the **DOMINANT.**
- The tone a 5th BELOW the tonic is called the **SUBDOMINANT.**

REMEMBER: SUB means "below" or "under." (SUBmarine, SUBway, etc.)

KEY OF C MAJOR:

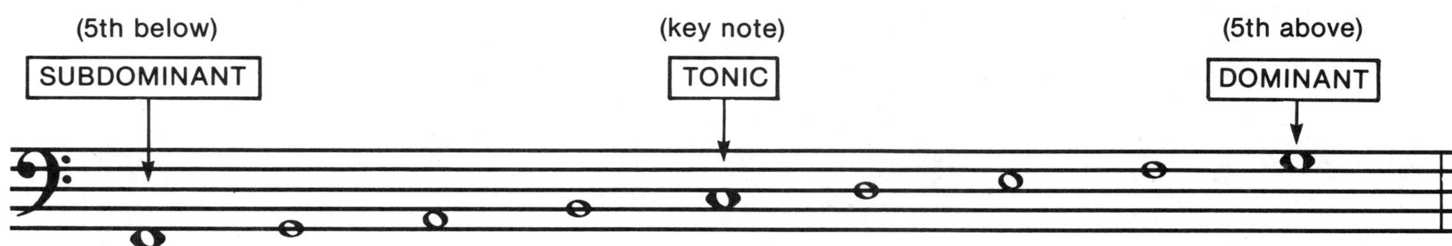

1. Write the SUBDOMINANT and DOMINANT degrees for each TONIC note given below:

KEY OF G MAJOR:

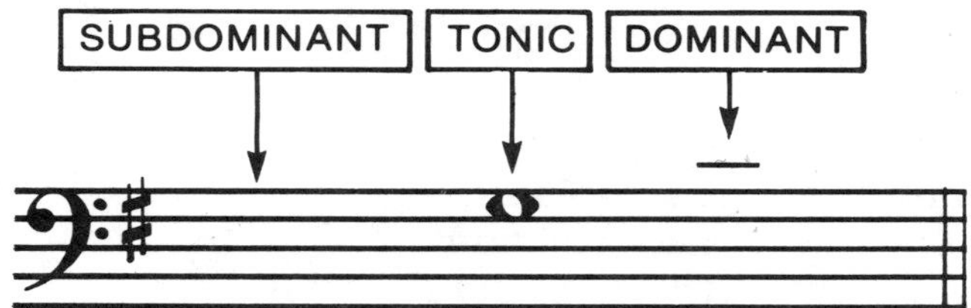

KEY OF D MAJOR:

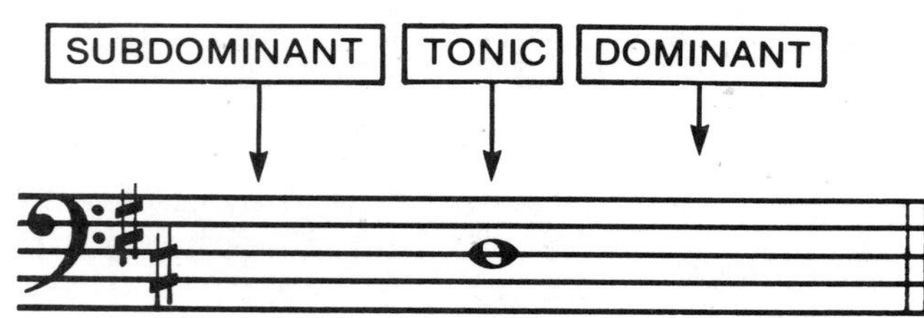

KEY OF F MAJOR:

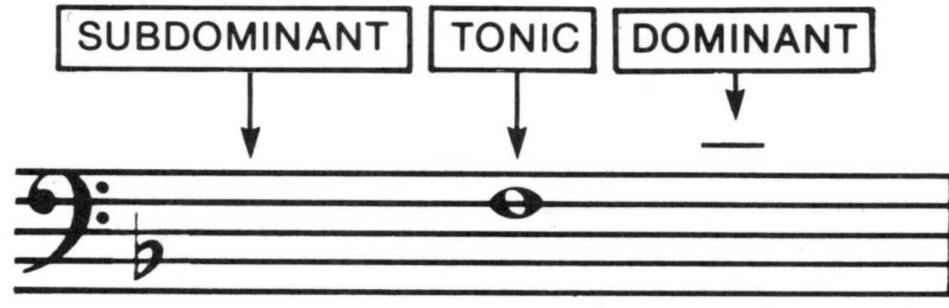

KEY OF B♭ MAJOR:

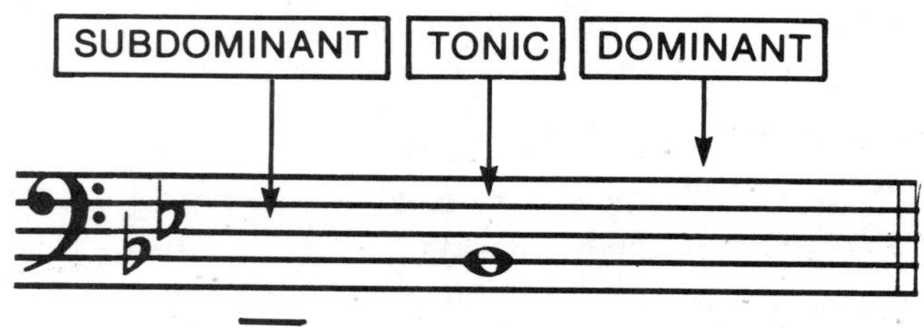

2. Write the answers in the blanks:

C is the TONIC in the key of ____ MAJOR.

C is the DOMINANT in the key of ____ MAJOR.

G is the DOMINANT in the key of ____ MAJOR.

C is the SUBDOMINANT in the key of ____ MAJOR.

Reviewing: The Circle of 5ths

Assign with the beginning of ADULT LESSON Book 3.

Using the **CIRCLE OF 5ths,** the TONIC, DOMINANT & SUBDOMINANT of any scale may be found quickly and easily.

- Take any letter on the circle as the key note or TONIC.
- The next letter clockwise is the DOMINANT.
- The next letter counter-clockwise is the SUBDOMINANT.

Example: Take C as the TONIC. The DOMINANT is G. The SUBDOMINANT is F.

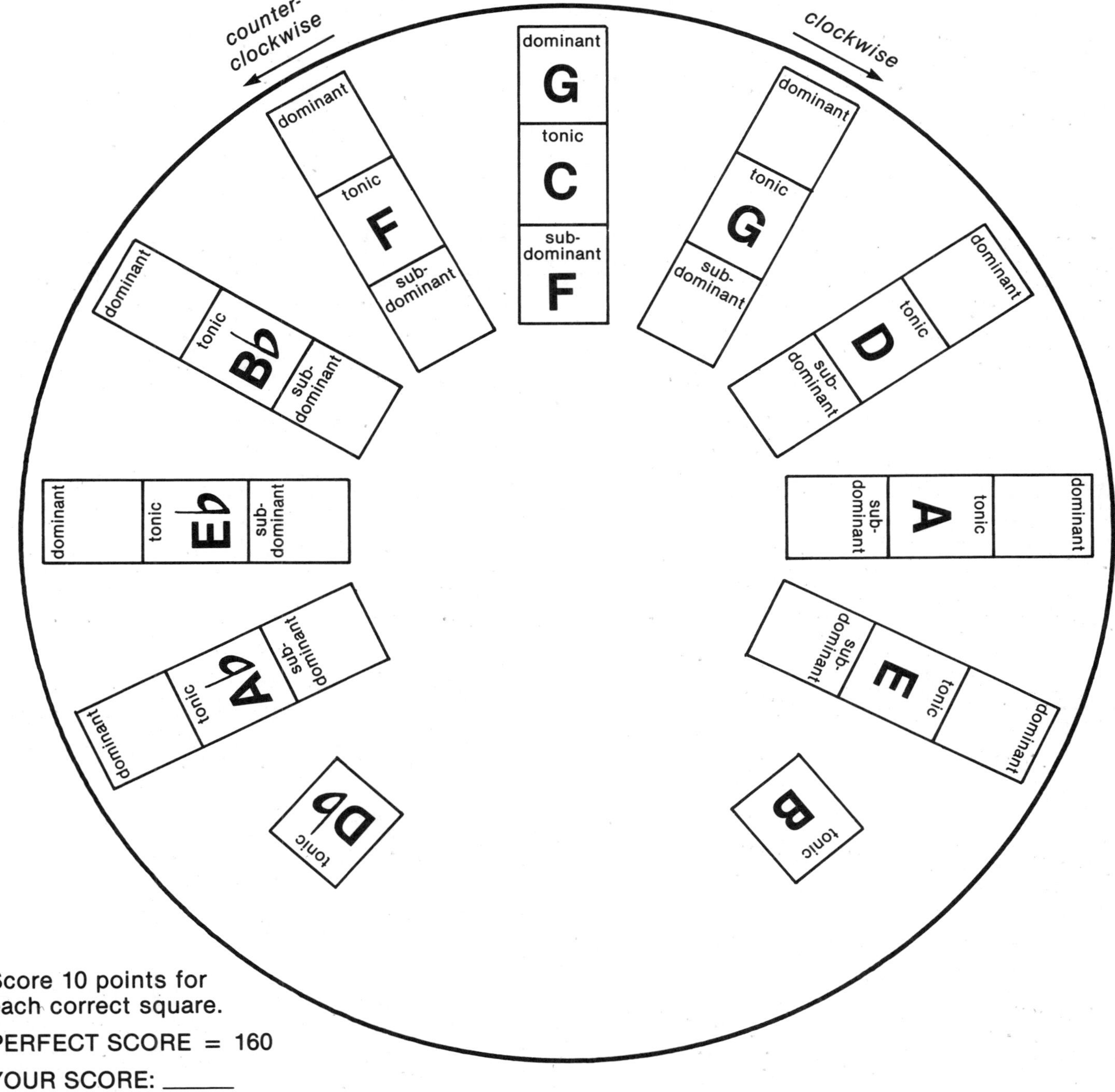

Score 10 points for each correct square.

PERFECT SCORE = 160

YOUR SCORE: ______

1. Write the DOMINANT note for each given TONIC in the square ABOVE it, turning the circle as you write. The answer will be the same as the next tonic note clockwise.
2. Write the SUBDOMINANT note for each given TONIC in the square BELOW it, turning the circle as you write. The answer will be the same as the next tonic note counter-clockwise.

The squares above and below C are filled in as examples.

Assign with pages 6–7.

REMEMBER: The DOMINANT is the 5th tone ABOVE the TONIC.

C MAJOR SCALE:

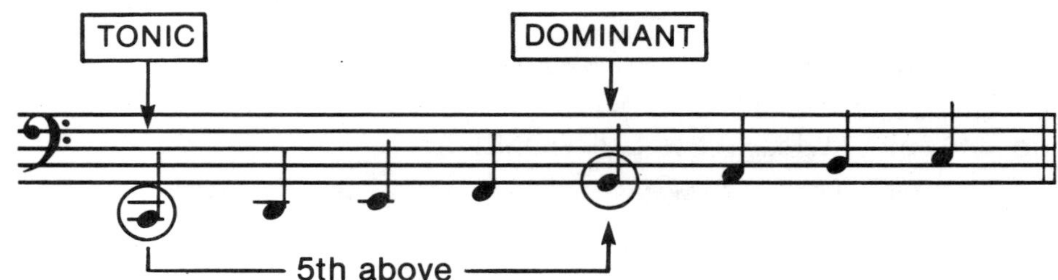

In the 5 scales below:

1. Circle all the TONIC notes.
2. Circle all the DOMINANT notes.

C MAJOR SCALE

G MAJOR SCALE

D MAJOR SCALE

F MAJOR SCALE

B♭ MAJOR SCALE

Assign with pages 6–7.

REMEMBER: The SUBDOMINANT is the 5th tone BELOW the TONIC.

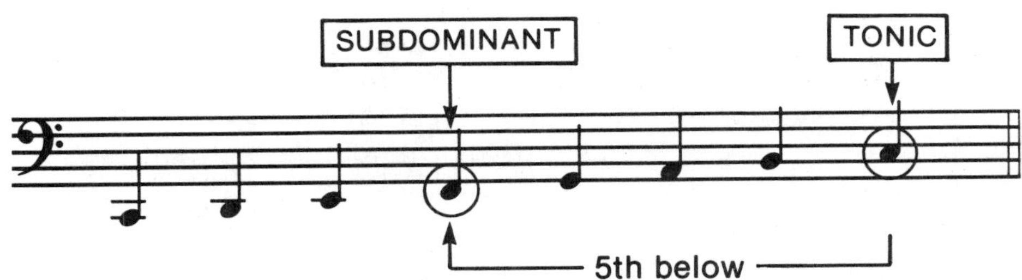

1. Circle all the SUBDOMINANT notes in the 5 scales on page 4.
2. Play each circled note, saying the name of the scale degree ("tonic," "subdominant" or "dominant").

THE SCALE DEGREES ARE NUMBERED WITH ROMAN NUMERALS.

TONIC = I DOMINANT = V SUBDOMINANT = IV

> **IMPORTANT!**
> The subdominant is numbered IV because of its position in the scale.
> It is NOT called "subdominant" because it is just below the dominant.
> It is called "subdominant" because it is the same distance BELOW the tonic as the dominant is ABOVE the tonic!

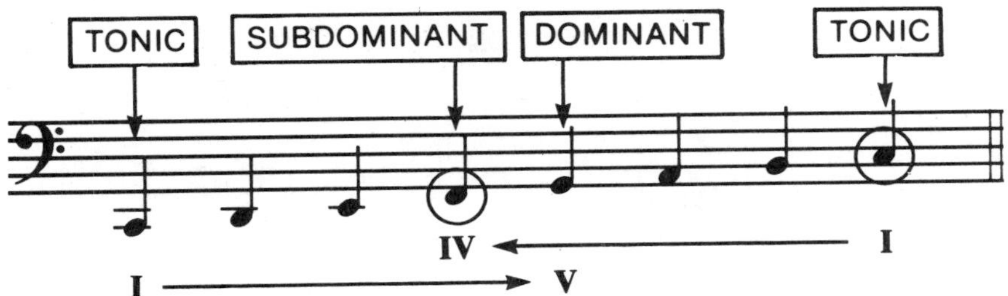

In the 4 scales below:

1. Write I below each TONIC note.
2. Write V below each DOMINANT note.
3. Write IV below each SUBDOMINANT note.

4. On page 4, write I below each TONIC NOTE, V below each DOMINANT note, and IV below each SUBDOMINANT note.

Assign with pages 8–9.

More Scale Degrees: Mediant & Submediant

- The **MEDIANT** is the 3rd degree ABOVE the TONIC (MIDWAY between the tonic and dominant).
- The **SUBMEDIANT** is the 3rd BELOW the TONIC (MIDWAY between the tonic and subdominant.)

Mediant is a Latin word meaning "in the middle."

KEY OF C MAJOR:

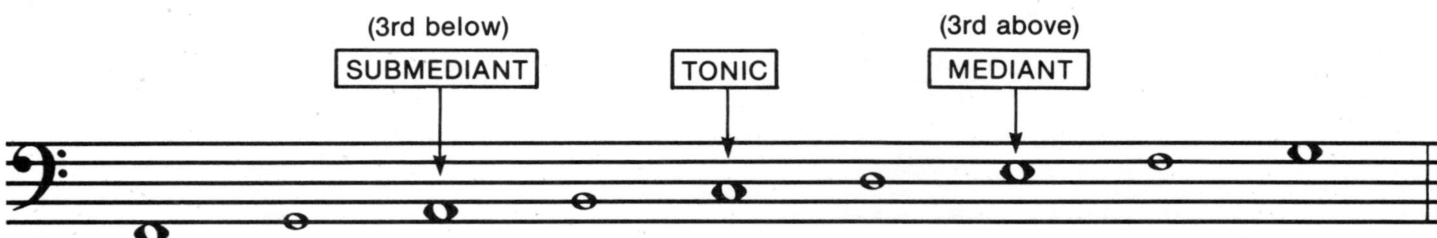

1. Write the SUBMEDIANT and MEDIANT degrees for each TONIC note given below:

KEY OF G MAJOR:

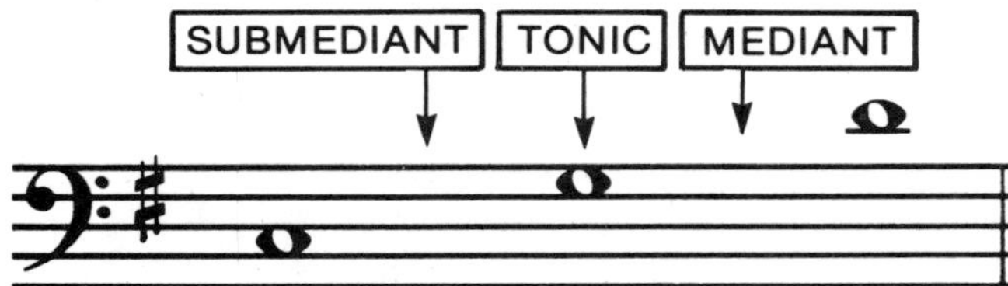

KEY OF D MAJOR:

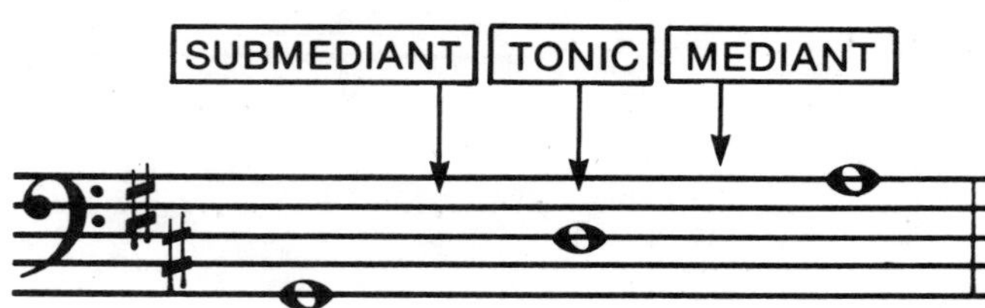

KEY OF F MAJOR:

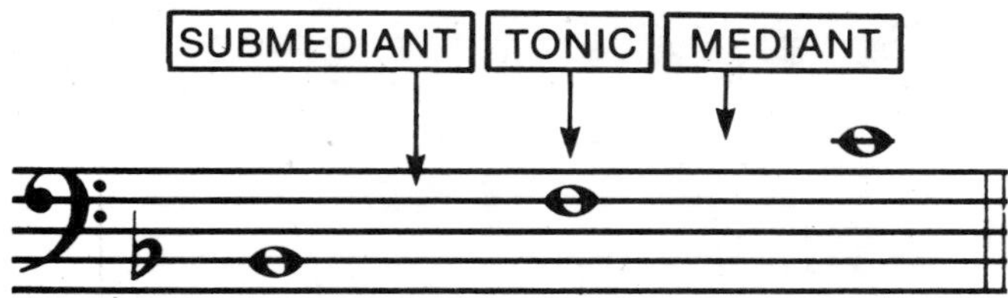

KEY OF B♭ MAJOR:

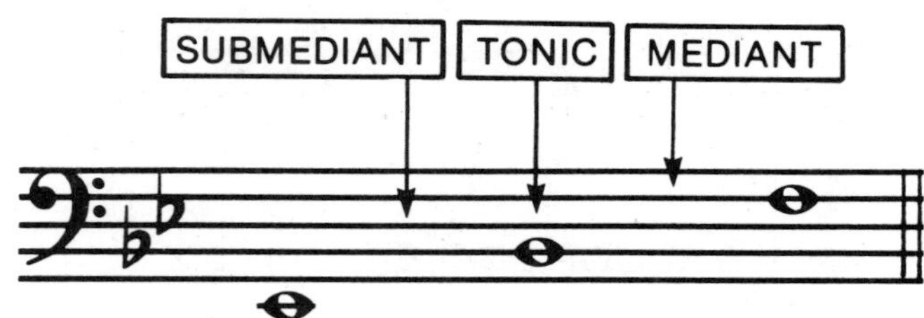

2. Write the answers in the blanks:

A is the MEDIANT in the key of ____ MAJOR. A is the DOMINANT in the key of ____ MAJOR.

A is the SUBMEDIANT in the key of ____ MAJOR. A is the TONIC in the key of ____ MAJOR.

Assign with pages 8–9.

REMEMBER: The MEDIANT is MIDWAY between the TONIC and DOMINANT.

C MAJOR SCALE:

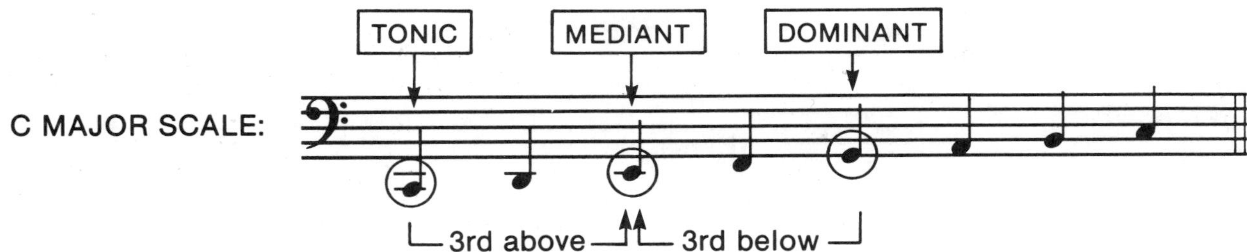

In the scales below:

1. Circle all the TONIC notes. 2. Circle all the DOMINANT notes. 3. Circle all the MEDIANT notes.

G MAJOR SCALE:

D MAJOR SCALE:

F MAJOR SCALE:

B♭ MAJOR SCALE:

Since the MEDIANT is the 3rd degree of the scale, it is given the Roman numeral III.

C MAJOR SCALE:

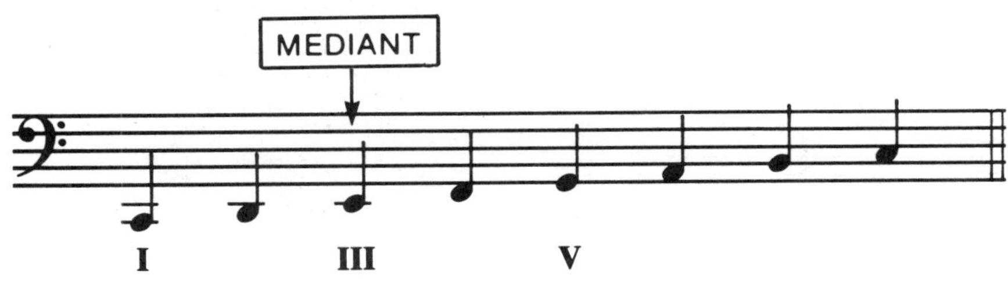

4. In the four scales under number 1 above, write I below each TONIC, III below each MEDIANT, and V below each DOMINANT.

Assign with pages 8–9.

REMEMBER: The SUBMEDIANT is MIDWAY between the SUBDOMINANT and the TONIC.

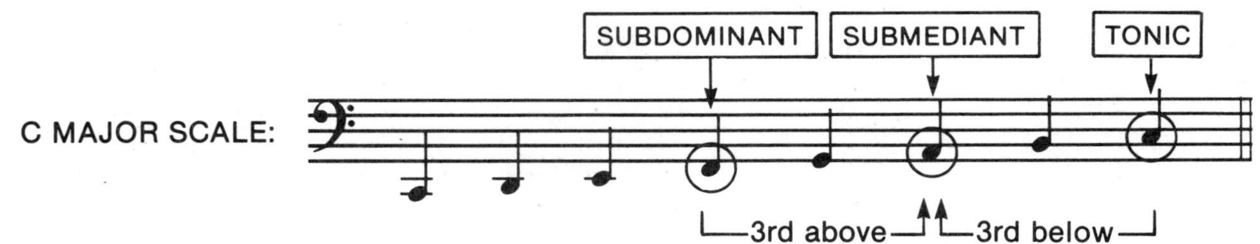

In the scales below:

1. Circle all the TONIC notes.
2. Circle all the SUBDOMINANT notes.
3. Circle all the SUBMEDIANT notes.

G MAJOR SCALE:

D MAJOR SCALE:

F MAJOR SCALE:

B♭ MAJOR SCALE:

Since the SUBMEDIANT is the 6th degree of the scale, it is given the Roman numeral VI.

C MAJOR SCALE:

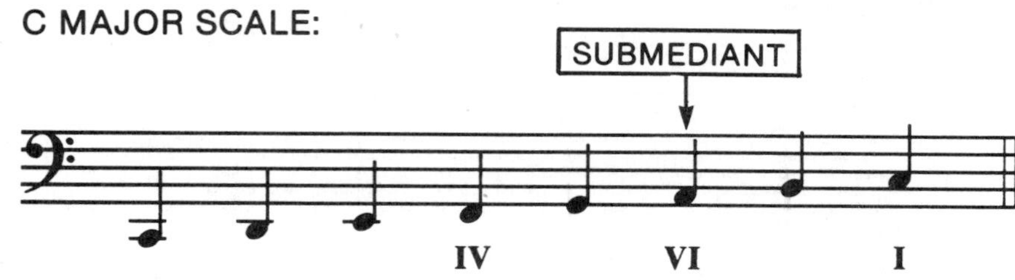

4. In the four scales under 1 above, write I below each TONIC, IV below each SUBDOMINANT, and VI below each SUBMEDIANT.

Assign with pages 10–11.

More Scale Degrees: Supertonic & Leading Tone

- The **SUPERTONIC** is the 2nd degree ABOVE the TONIC.
- The **LEADING TONE** is the 2nd degree BELOW the TONIC.

The LEADING TONE is sometimes called the SUBTONIC. "Leading tone" is most often used, since the note has a strong tendency to "lead" to the TONIC, as it does in an ascending scale.

NOTE: The SUPERTONIC is always a WHOLE STEP above the tonic.
The LEADING TONE is always a HALF STEP below the tonic.

KEY OF C MAJOR:

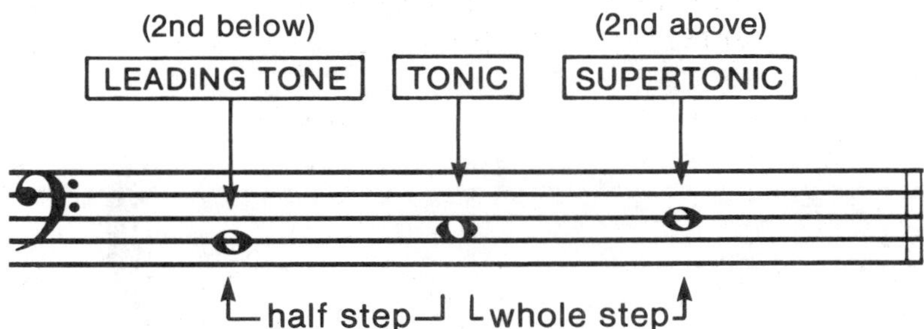

1. Write the LEADING TONE and SUPERTONIC degrees for each TONIC note:

KEY OF G MAJOR:

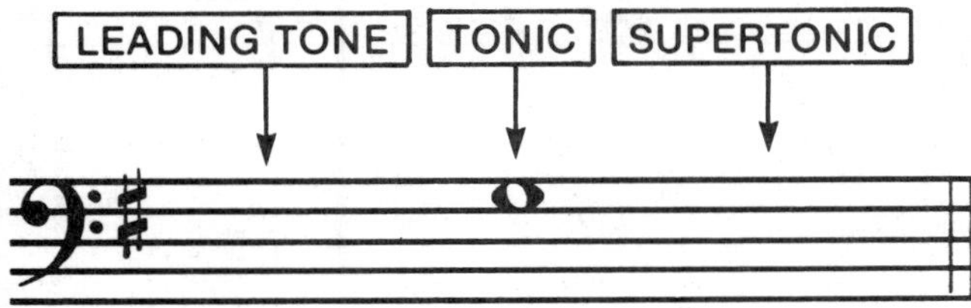

KEY OF D MAJOR:

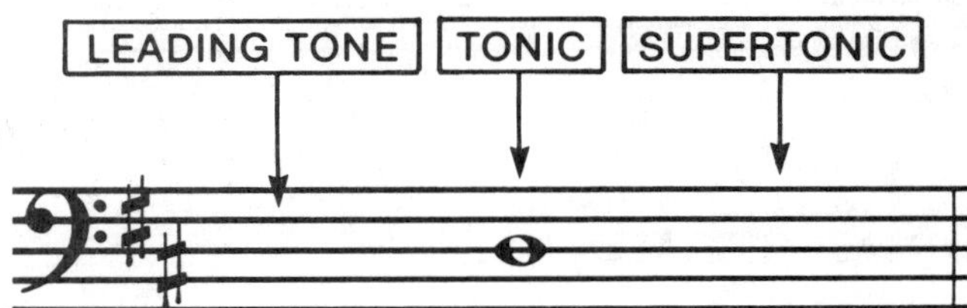

KEY OF F MAJOR:

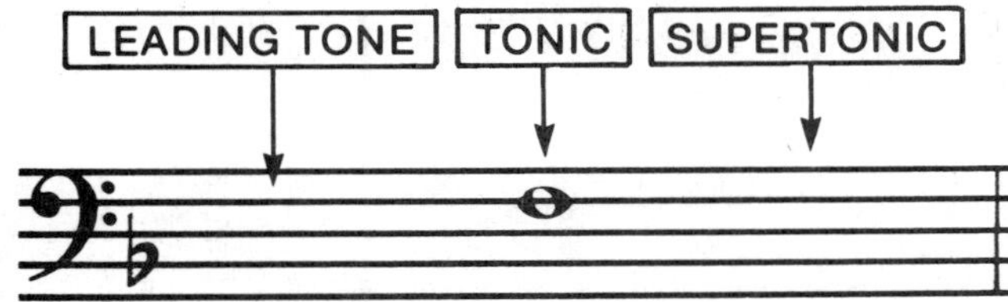

KEY OF B♭ MAJOR:

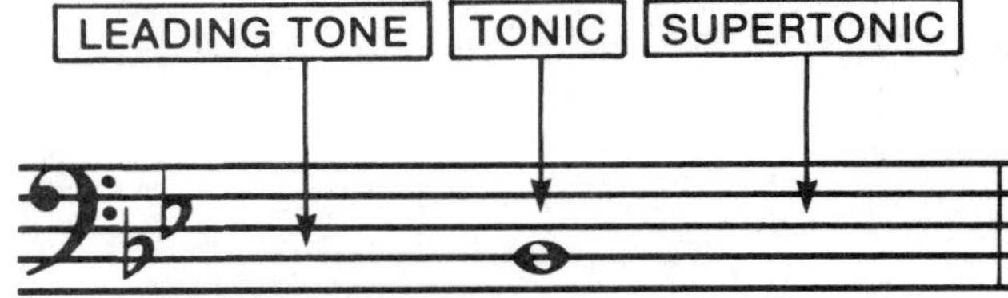

2. Write the answers in the blanks:

A is the LEADING TONE in the key of ____ MAJOR. A is the SUPERTONIC in the key of ____ MAJOR.

E is the LEADING TONE in the key of ____ MAJOR. E is the SUPERTONIC in the key of ____ MAJOR.

Assign with pages 10–11.

**REMEMBER: The SUPERTONIC is one WHOLE STEP ABOVE the TONIC.
The LEADING TONE is one HALF STEP BELOW the TONIC.**

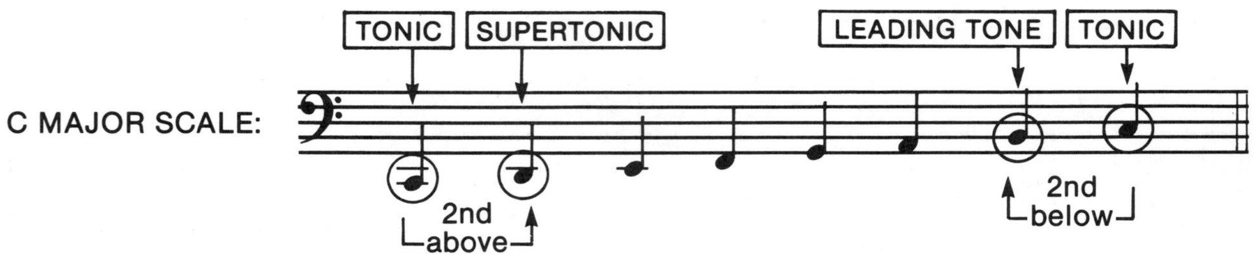

In the scales below:

1. Circle all the TONIC NOTES.
2. Circle all the SUPERTONIC notes.
3. Circle all the LEADING TONES.

G MAJOR SCALE:

D MAJOR SCALE:

F MAJOR SCALE:

B♭ MAJOR SCALE:

**Since the SUPERTONIC is the 2nd degree of the scale, it is given the Roman numeral II.
The LEADING TONE is the 7th degree, so it is given the numeral VII.**

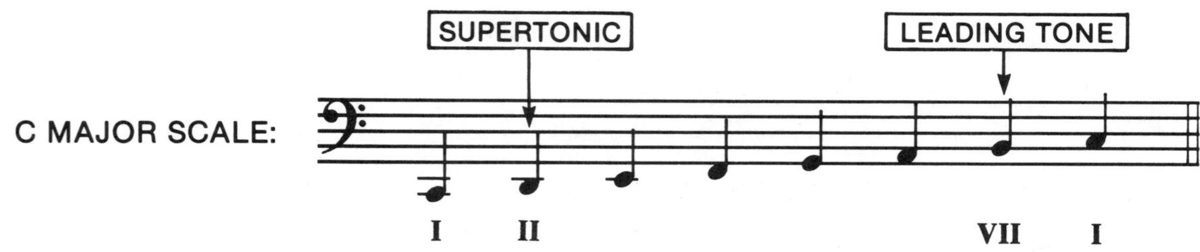

4. In the four scales under 1 above, write I below each TONIC, II below each SUPERTONIC, and VII below each LEADING TONE.

Assign with pages 10–11.

Reviewing the Scale Degrees

You now know the names of all the scale degrees. Arranged in order, the names are:

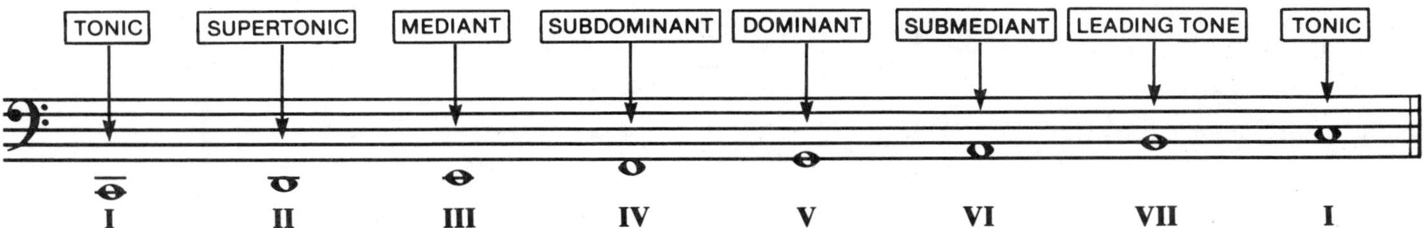

Be sure to remember that the degree names were derived from the following arrangement, in which the TONIC is taken as the center tone:

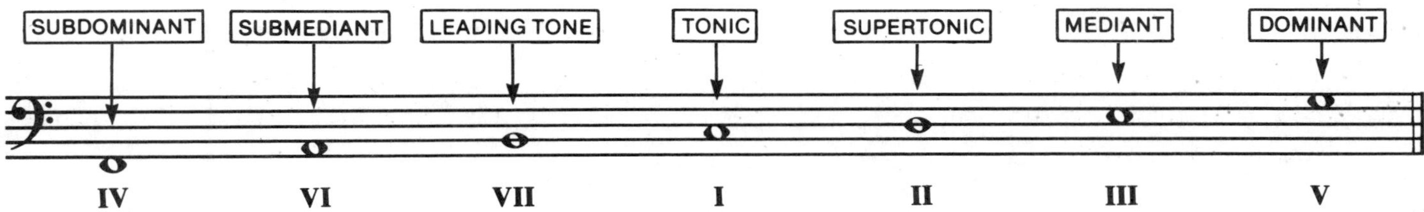

1. Write the degree names in the boxes above the notes.
2. Write the degree numbers (Roman numerals) in the boxes below the notes.

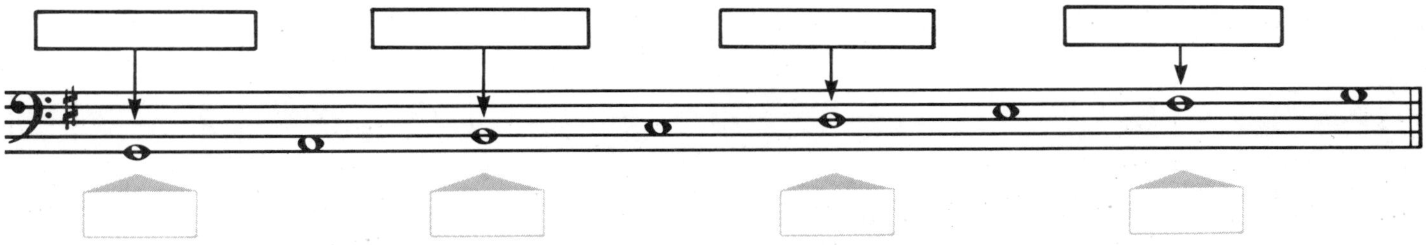

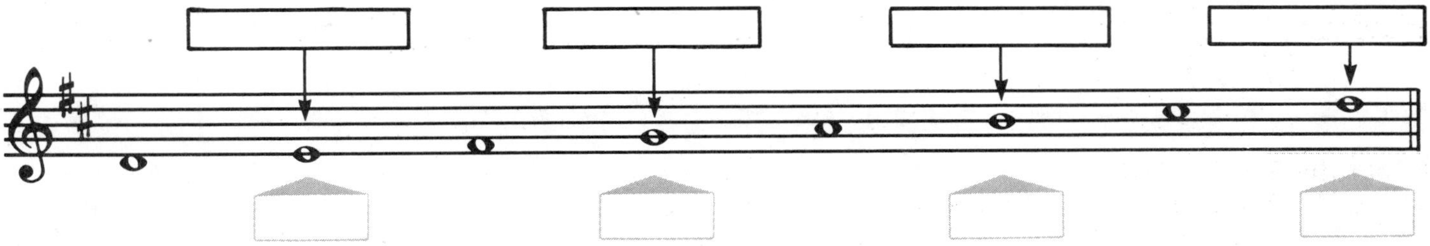

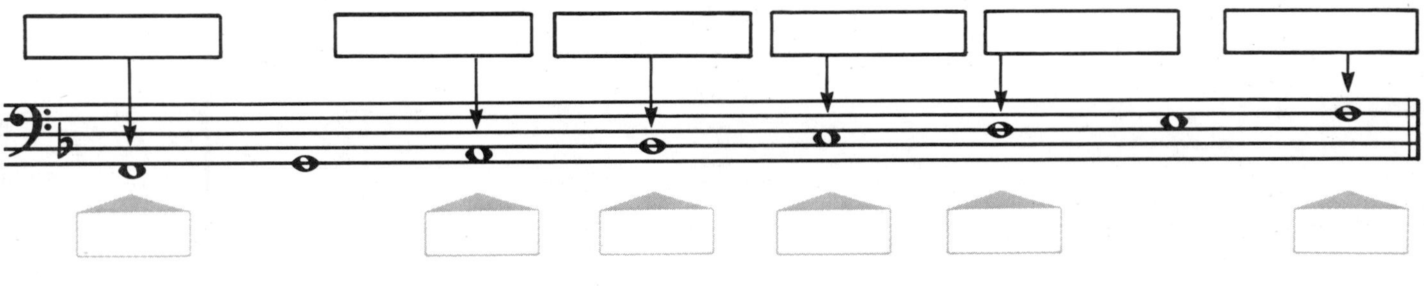

Assign with pages 12–13.

Alberti Bass

This style of LH accompaniment gets its name from the 16th Century Italian composer, Domenico Alberti, who used it in many of his compositions. It was used also by Haydn, Mozart, Clementi and Beethoven, along with many other composers of the Classical period.

The first line of the music below shows a basic I-IV-V7 progression. The 2nd and 3rd lines introduce the corresponding Alberti bass in $\frac{4}{4}$ and $\frac{3}{4}$ time.

Play the following several times:

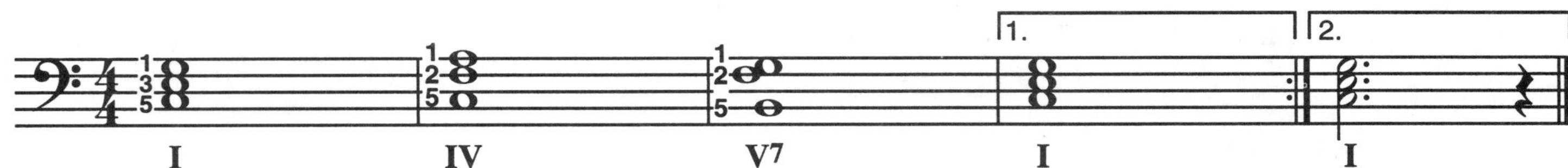

Alberti bass in $\frac{4}{4}$ time:

Alberti bass in $\frac{3}{4}$ time:

G MAJOR PROGRESSION:

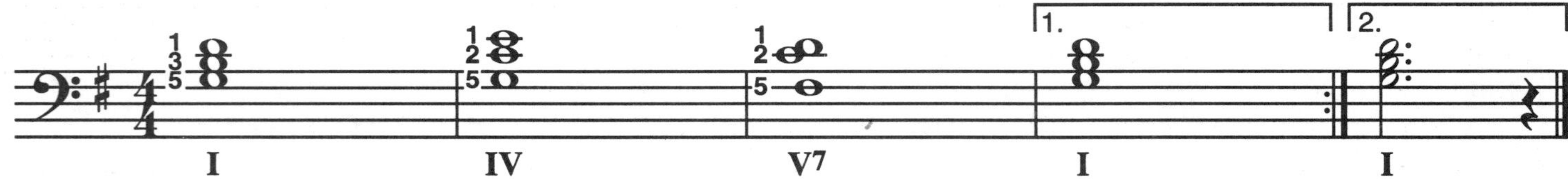

Write in the missing measures of Alberti bass, then play several times:

Alberti bass in $\frac{4}{4}$ time:

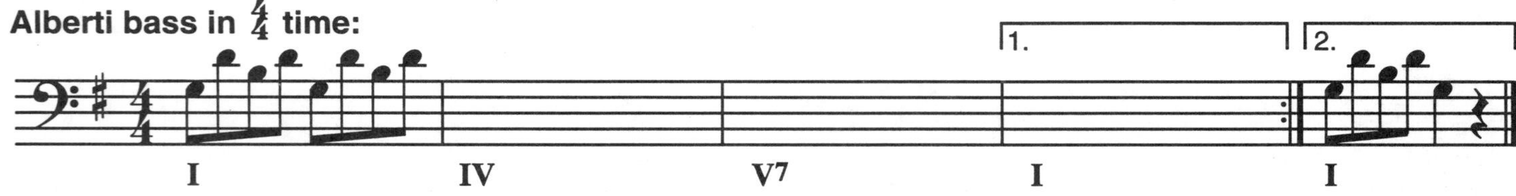

Alberti bass in $\frac{3}{4}$ time:

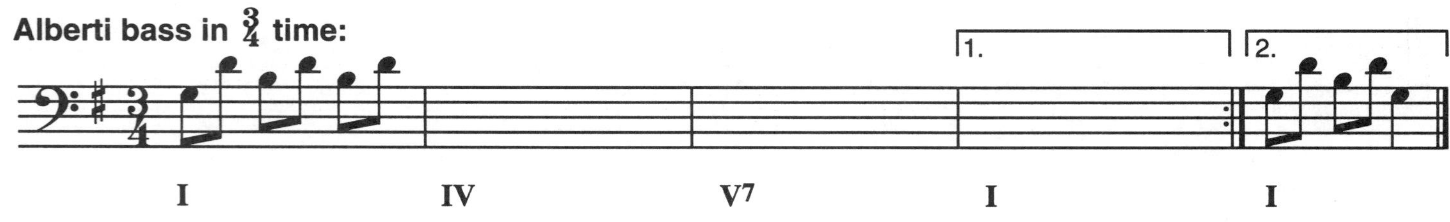

Assign with pages 12–13.

Alberti Bass in 4/4 Time in C Major

1. Write in the missing Alberti bass in 4/4 time.
2. Play, carefully observing phrasing and dynamics.

Assign with pages 12–13.

Alberti Bass in $\frac{3}{4}$ Time in G Major

1. Write in the missing Alberti bass in $\frac{3}{4}$ time. Repeat the previous measure unless there is a chord change indicated by a new Roman numeral.
2. Play, carefully observing phrasing and dynamics.

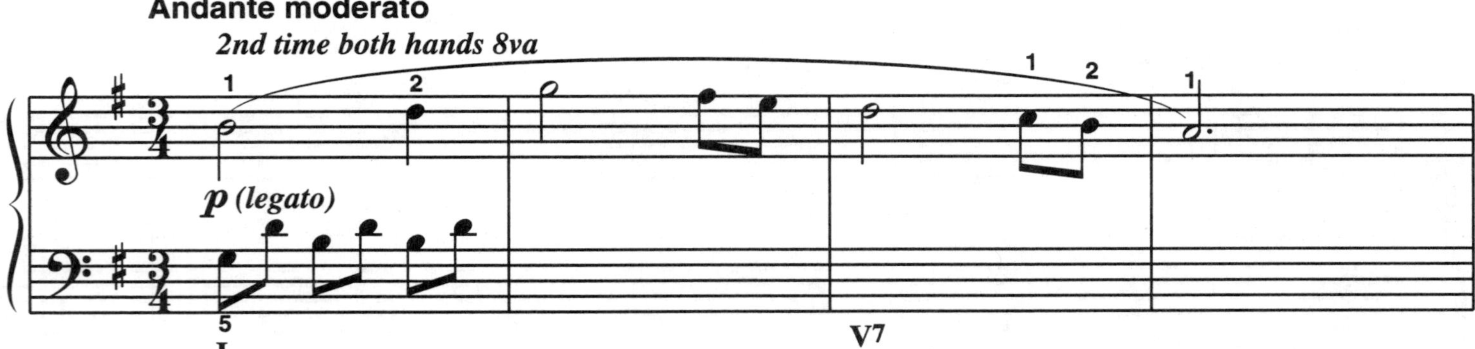

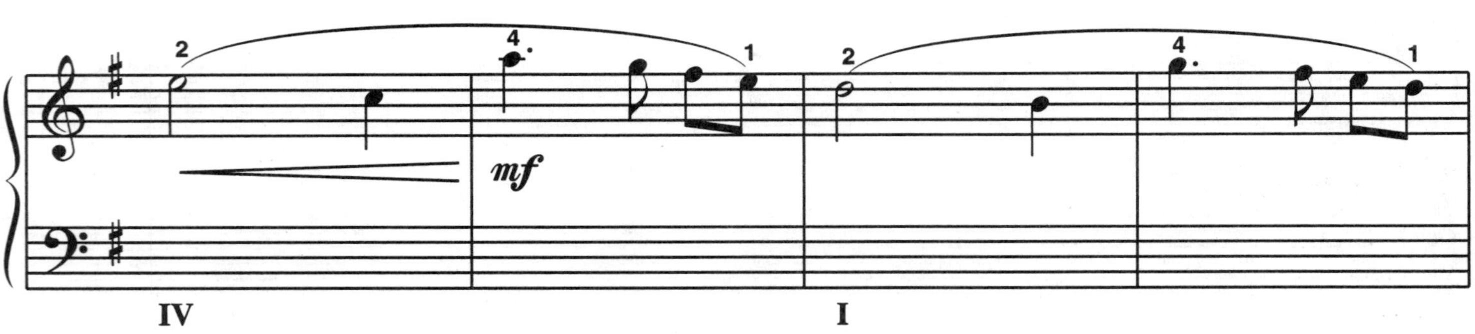

Assign with pages 14–15.

Alberti Bass in F Major

1. Play several times:

Alberti bass may be played in various broken chord configurations.

2. Play several times:

Sometimes the first LH note is held throughout the chord, for a special effect.

3. Play several times:

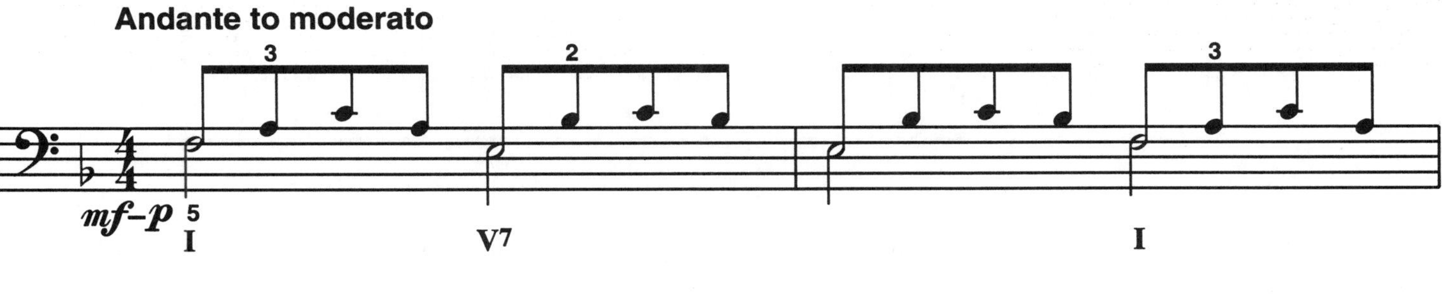

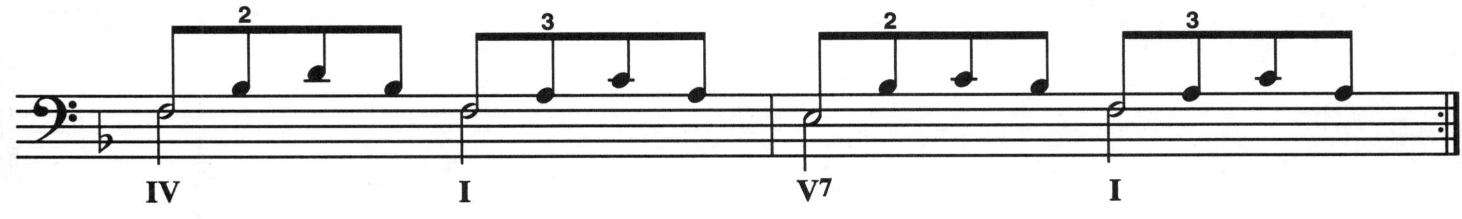

Assign with pages 16–17.

The Diminished Seventh Chord

Remember: The DOMINANT SEVENTH CHORD may be formed by adding one note to the major triad, a minor 3rd (3 half steps) above the 5th of the chord.

The DIMINISHED SEVENTH CHORD may be formed by lowering each note of the DOMINANT SEVENTH chord (V7) 1 half step, except the root, which remains the same.

C DOMINANT 7th (C7)

C DIMINISHED 7th (Cdim7)

1. The chords in the DOMINANT 7th column below are spelled correctly. Chords in the DIMINISHED 7th column are not. In the following exercise, change each **DOMINANT 7th** chord into a **DIMINISHED 7th** chord by lowering the 3rd, 5th, and 7th of the chord in the DIMINISHED 7th column. Use naturals, flats, and double flats. Each chord note *must* skip one letter of the musical alphabet. Remember: The double flat (𝄫) lowers a note ONE WHOLE STEP!

2. Play each DOMINANT 7th followed by the DIMINISHED 7th in the column on the right. Use RH 1 2 3 5 or LH 5 3 2 1, saying the name of each chord as you play it: "G DOMINANT 7th, G DIMINISHED 7th," etc.

(add the missing accidentals)

DOMINANT 7ths				DIMINISHED 7ths			
Root	3rd	5th	7th	Root	3rd	5th	7th
D	F♯	A	C	D	F	A	C
G	B	D	F	G	B	D	F
C	E	G	B♭	C	E	G	B
F	A	C	E♭	F	A	C	E
B♭	D	F	A♭	B♭	D	F	A
E♭	G	B♭	D♭	E♭	G	B	D
A♭	C	E♭	G♭	A♭	C	E	G

A DIMINISHED SEVENTH CHORD may also be formed on any given root by skipping the interval of a MINOR 3rd (3 HALF STEPS) between each note.

3. Play the following DIMINISHED 7th CHORDS, using R.H. 1 2 3 5. Check each chord to be sure that the interval between each note is a MINOR 3rd.

Assign with pages 16–17.

An Easy Way to Make ANY Diminished Seventh Chord

Here is a **QUICK** and **EASY** way to make **ANY** DIMINISHED 7th CHORD:

Choose any note as the **ROOT.**
Skip **3 HALF STEPS** for the **3rd.**
Skip **3 HALF STEPS** again for the **5th**.
Skip **3 HALF STEPS** again for the **7th.**

EXAMPLE: G dim 7th

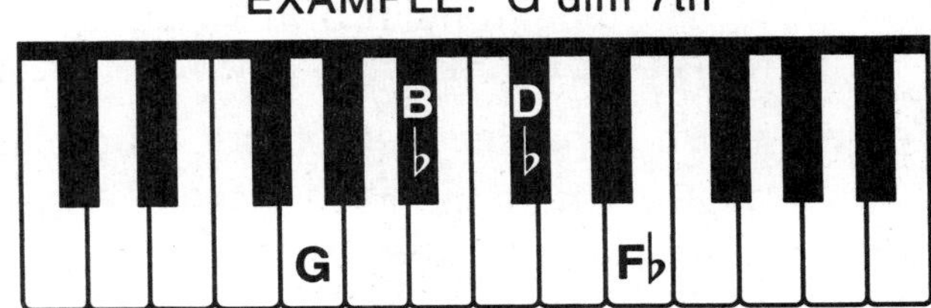

1. Play each of the following DIMINISHED 7th CHORDS in several places on the keyboard. Use **RH 1 2 3 5.** Repeat, using **LH 5 3 2 1.** Carefully note that there are exactly **3 HALF STEPS** between each of the four notes of each chord.

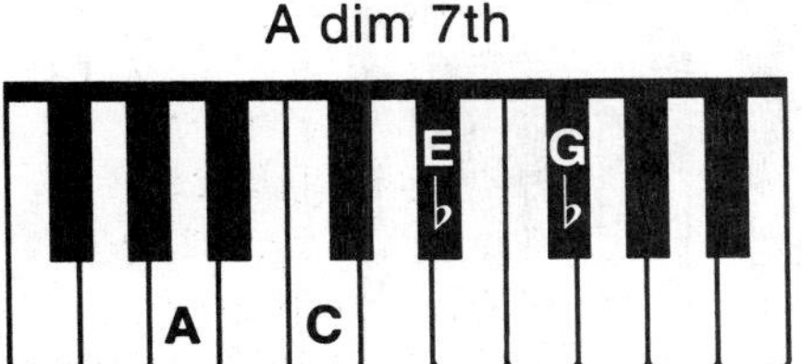

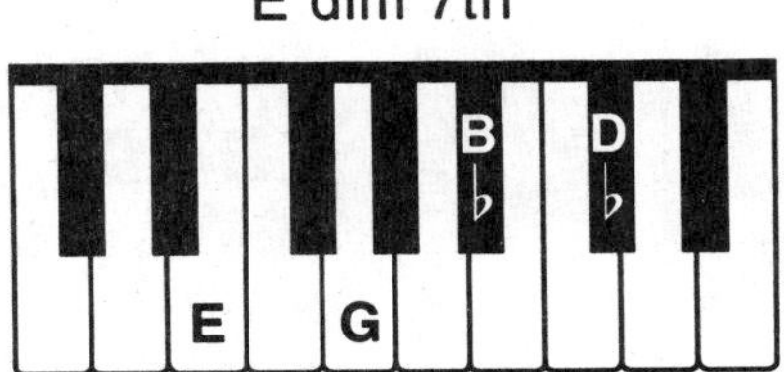

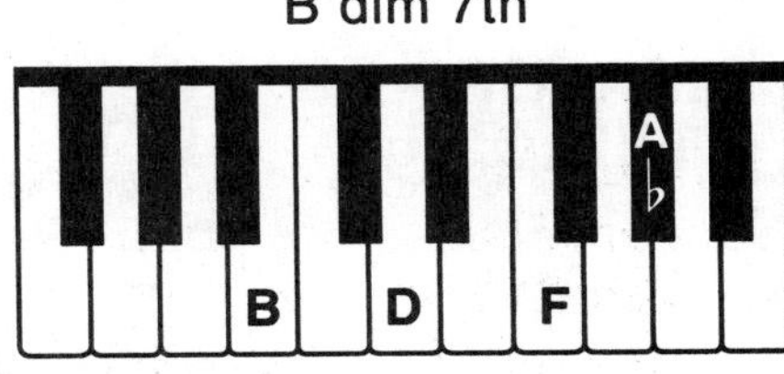

2. Build diminished 7th chords on each of the following keyboard diagrams, using the given note as the **ROOT** of the chord. Write the letter names of the **3rd, 5th** and **7th** on each keyboard.

To be sure you are spelling each chord correctly, use the 7th CHORD VOCABULARY (see page 46 in ADULT LESSON BOOK TWO).

REMEMBER: Each chord note must skip one letter of the musical alphabet.

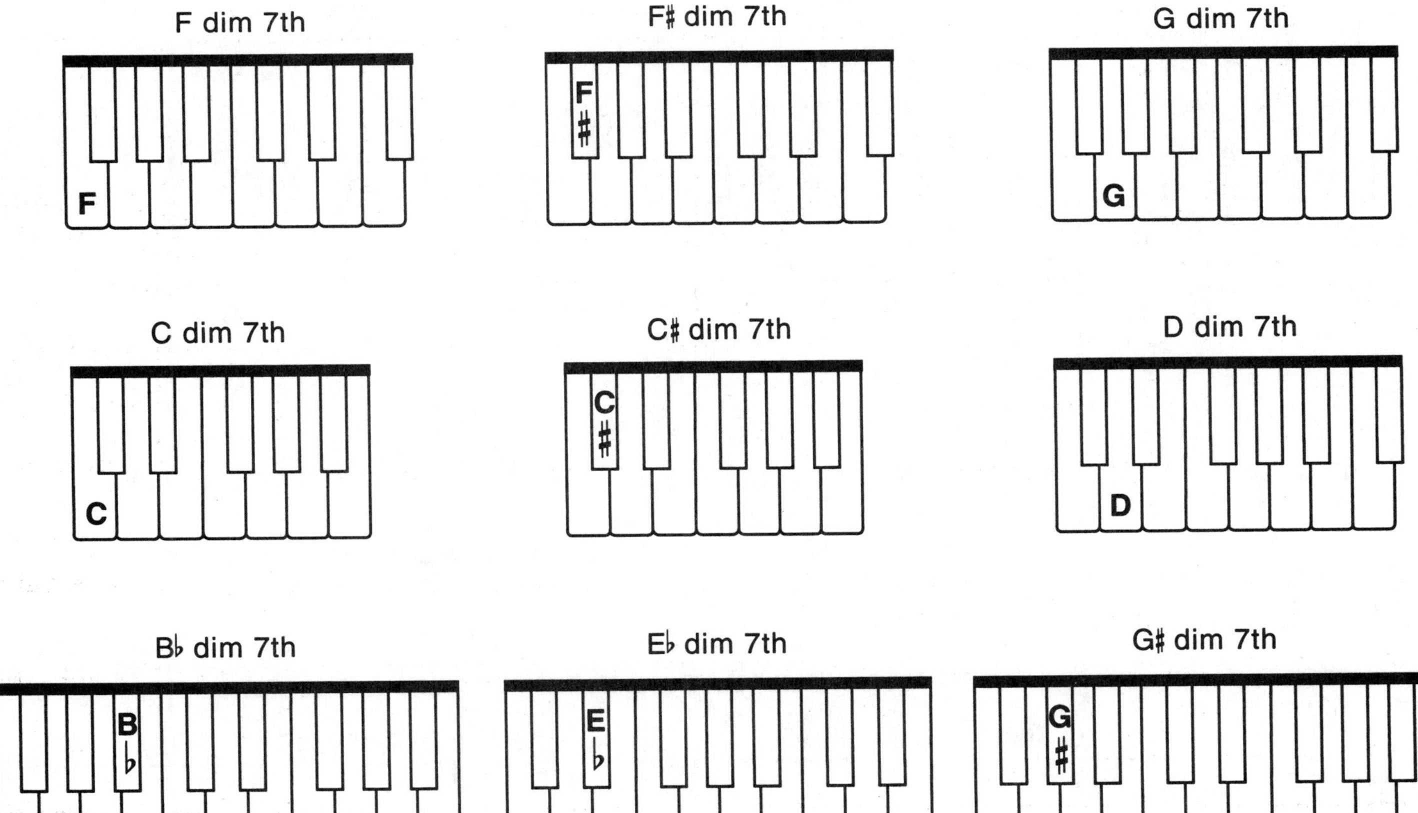

Assign with pages 18–28.

Reviewing: Major & Minor Triads

You have learned to identify MAJOR and MINOR triads in ROOT POSITION as follows:

- MAJOR triads consist of a MAJOR 3rd and a PERFECT 5th.
- MINOR triads consist of a MINOR 3rd and a PERFECT 5th.

} Intervals above the ROOT.

You may also consider these triads as consisting of "stacked 3rds":

- MAJOR triads consist of a MAJOR 3rd plus a MINOR 3rd.
- MINOR triads consist of a MINOR 3rd plus a MAJOR 3rd.

} Intervals from note to note.

REMEMBER: a MAJOR 3rd has 4 half steps; a MINOR 3rd has 3 half steps.

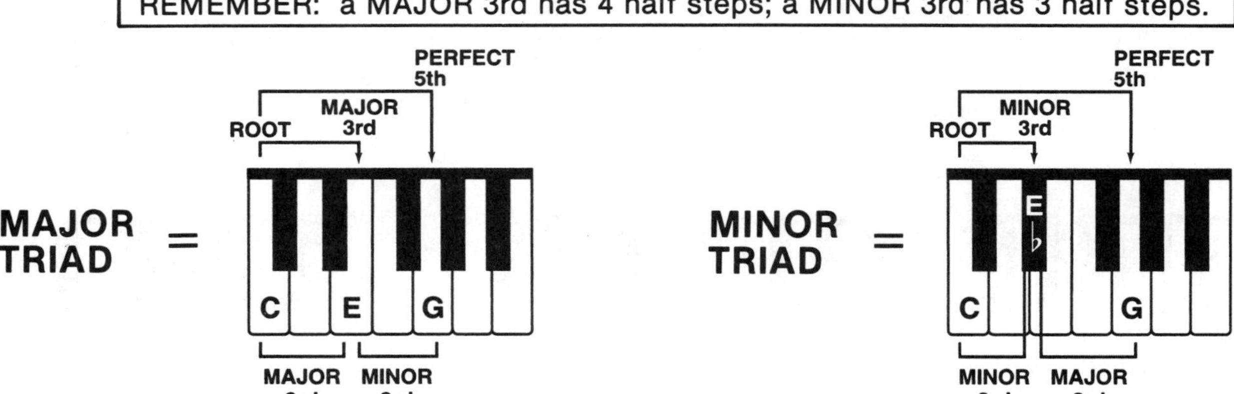

1. In the box below each diagram, write "MAJOR" for each major triad, and "MINOR" for each minor triad, as shown in the first example.

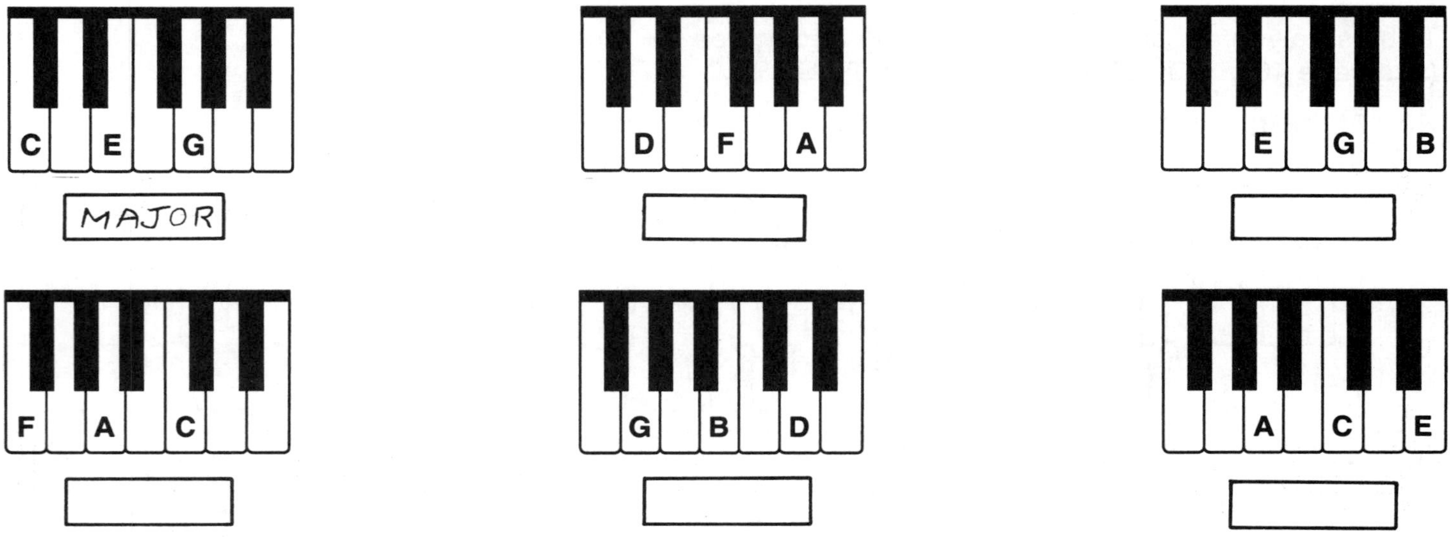

TRIADS BUILT ON THE FIRST SIX DEGREES OF THE C MAJOR SCALE

2. In the box just below the name of each scale degree, write "MAJOR" if the triad is major, and "MINOR" if the triad is minor.
3. In the lower row of boxes write the ROMAN NUMERALS for each scale degree. Use a LARGE numeral if the triad is MAJOR, and SMALL numeral if it is MINOR.

TONIC	SUPERTONIC	MEDIANT	SUBDOMINANT	DOMINANT	SUBMEDIANT
MAJOR					
I					

Assign with pages 30–35.

Two-Octave Arpeggios

The word ARPEGGIO comes from the Italian *arpeggiare,* which means "to play upon a harp." This refers to playing the notes of a chord in a broken fashion, one after another, as one does when playing a harp.

TWO-OCTAVE ARPEGGIOS on triads containing ALL WHITE KEYS are fingered as follows:

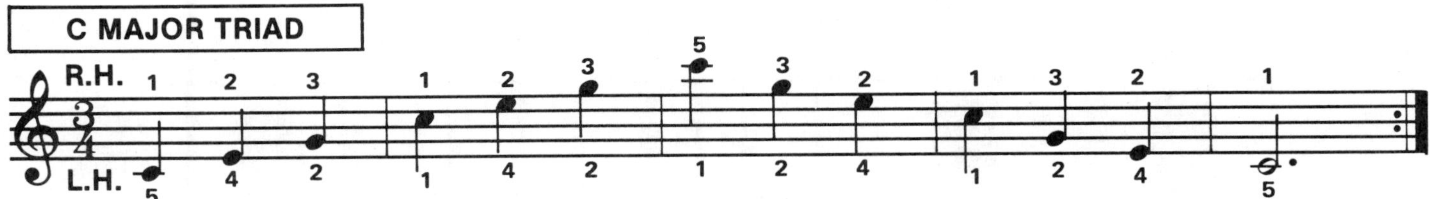

1. Write the NAME of the arpeggiated triad in the box above the beginning of each staff below.
2. Write the R.H. fingering ABOVE each note.
3. Write the L.H. fingering BELOW each note.
4. Play with R.H. as written.
5. Play with L.H. two octaves lower than written.

R.H.
L.H.

R.H.
L.H.

R.H.
L.H.

R.H.
L.H.

R.H.
L.H.

The A Major Scale

Assign with pages 36–37.

1. Write the letter names of the notes of the A MAJOR SCALE, from *left to right,* on the keyboard below. Be sure the WHOLE STEPS & HALF STEPS are correct!

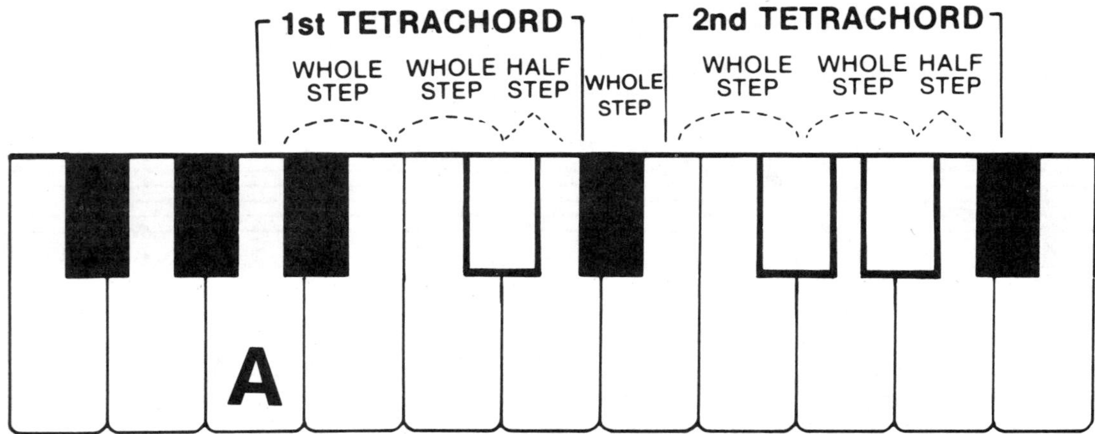

2. Complete the tetrachord beginning on A. Write one note over each finger number.

3. Complete the tetrachord beginning on E. Write one note over each finger number.

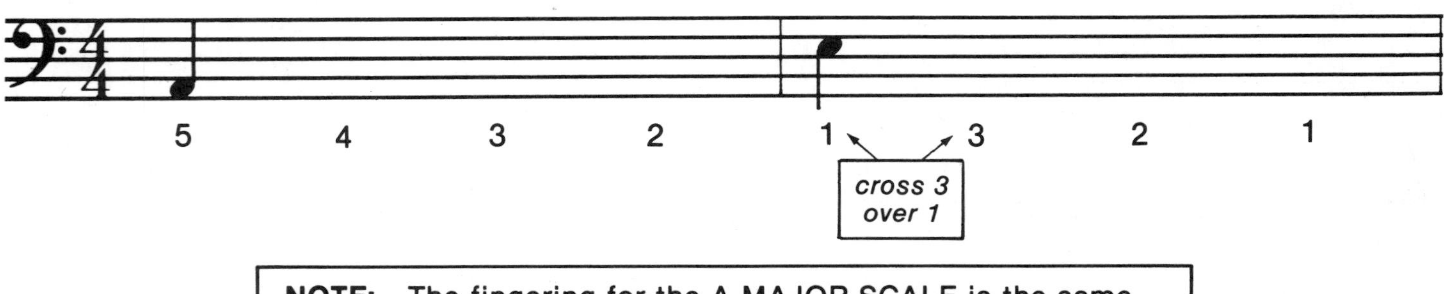

NOTE: The fingering for the A MAJOR SCALE is the same as for the C MAJOR, G MAJOR, & D MAJOR SCALES.

4. Write the fingering UNDER each note of the following L.H. scale. Cross 3 over 1 ascending. Cross 1 under 3 descending.

5. Play with L.H.

6. Write the fingering OVER each note of the following R.H. scale. Cross 1 under 3 ascending. Cross 3 over 1 descending.

7. Play with R.H.

The Primary Chords in A Major

Assign with pages 38–39.

In MAJOR KEYS: the **I chord** is the TONIC CHORD (major).
the **IV chord** is the SUBDOMINANT CHORD (major).
the **V7 chord** is the DOMINANT 7th CHORD.

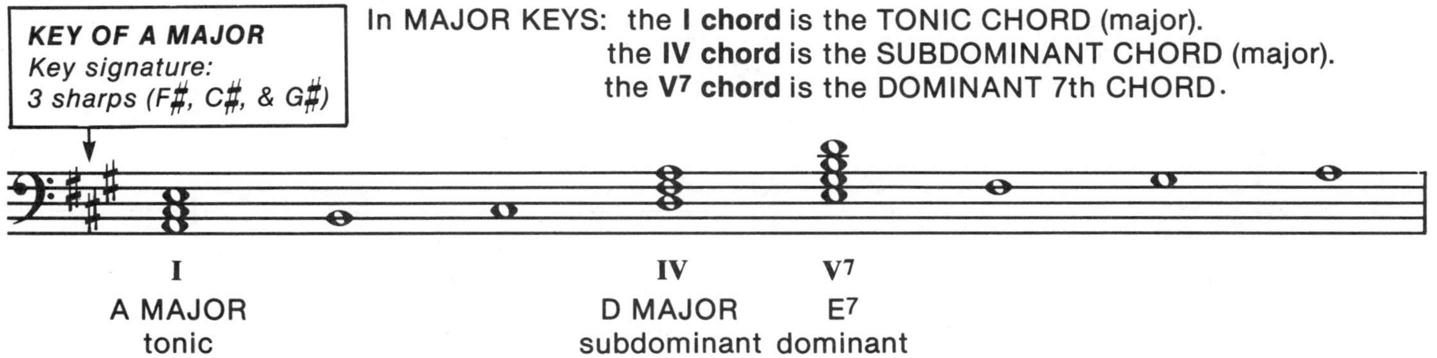

The following positions are often used for smooth progressions:

1. Add the A MAJOR key signature to each staff below.
2. Write the PRIMARY CHORDS in A MAJOR, using the above positions.

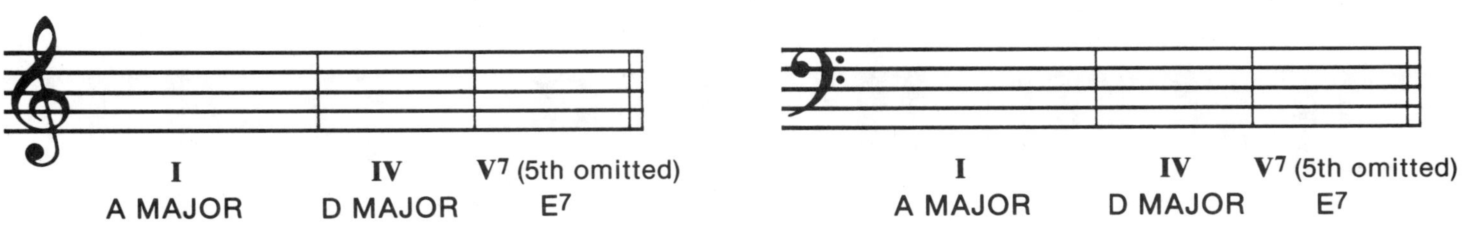

3. Write the ROMAN NUMERALS (**I, IV, V7**) in the boxes below.
4. Play.

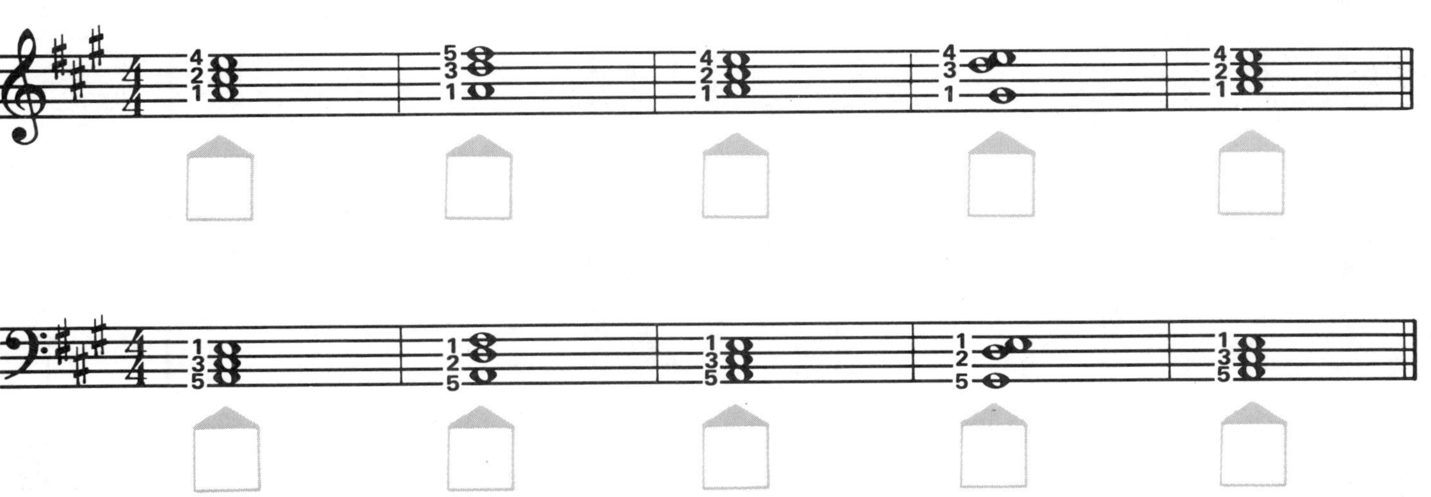

*Fingering for chords varies depending on the context of the chord. 1 2 4 is used here for the A major triad because it allows a smooth progression to the next chord.

Assign with pages 38–39.

The Primary Chords in A Major—All Positions

1. In the blank measures after each ROOT POSITION chord, write the 2 INVERSIONS of the chord.

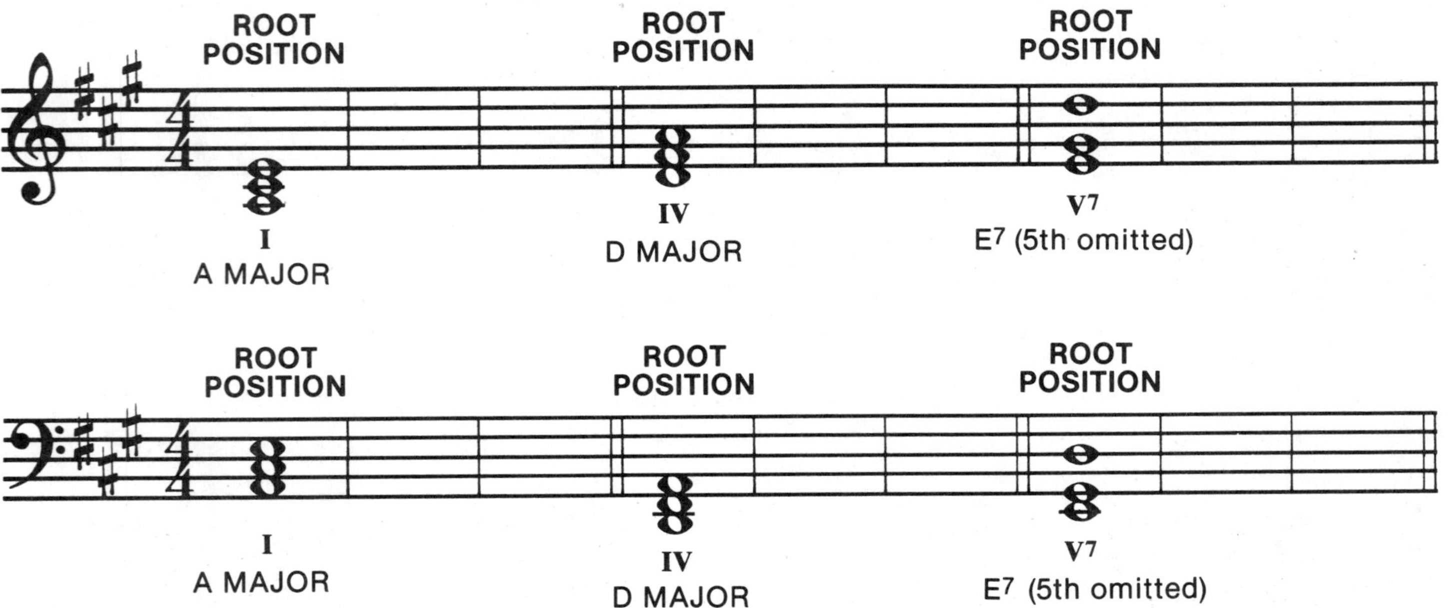

2. On the 2 keyboards to the right of each ROOT POSITION chord, write the letter names showing the 2 inversions of the chord.

ROOT POSITION — **INVERSIONS**

L.H. 5 3 1 R.H. 1 2 4 — L.H. 5 3 1 R.H. 1 2 5 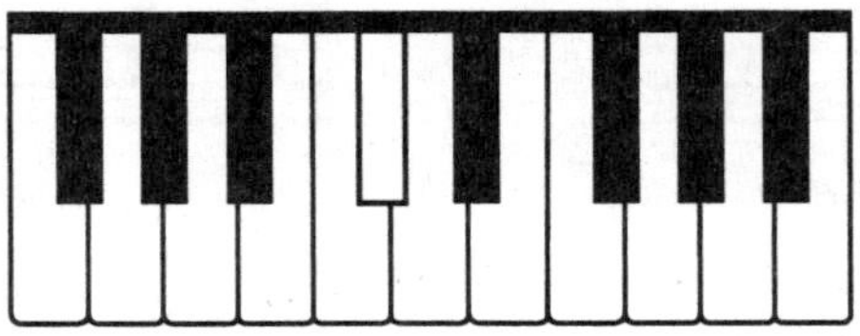 — L.H. 5 2 1 R.H. 1 3 5

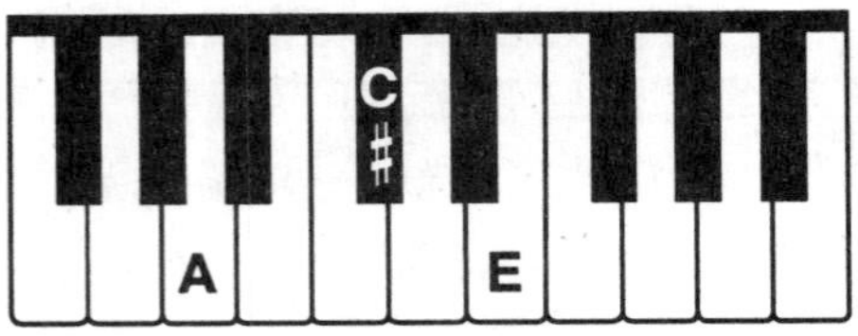

A C# E

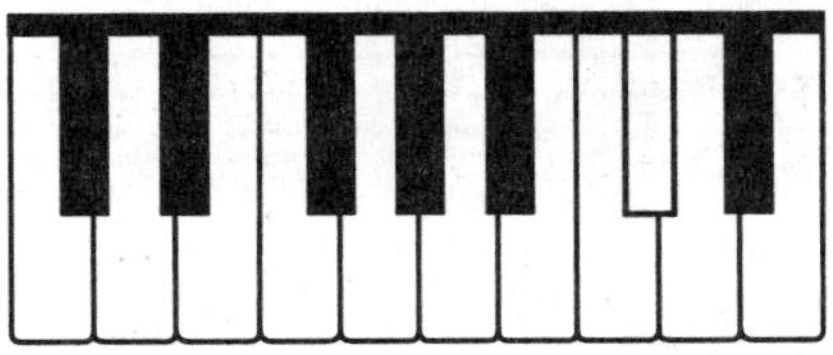

I A MAJOR (tonic)

L.H. 5 3 1 R.H. 1 3 5 — L.H. 5 3 1 R.H. 1 2 5 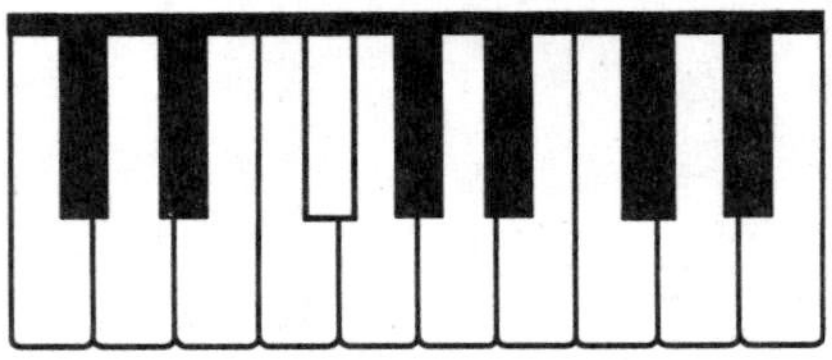 — L.H. 5 2 1 R.H. 1 3 5

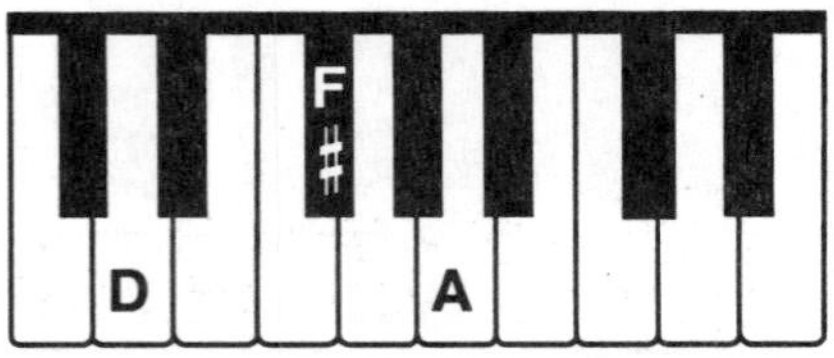

D F# A

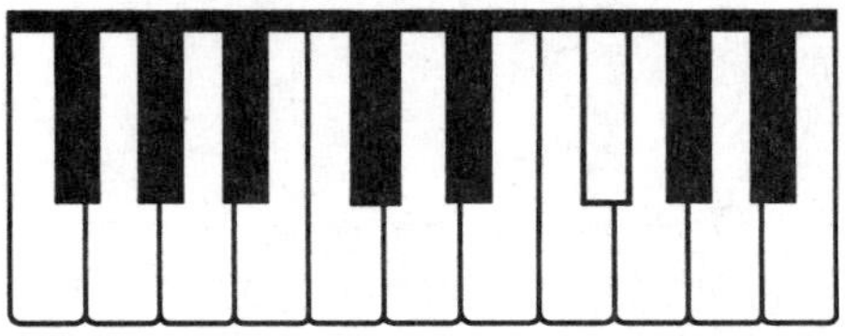

IV D MAJOR (subdominant)

L.H. 5 3 1 R.H. 1 2 5 — L.H. 5 2 1 R.H. 1 4 5 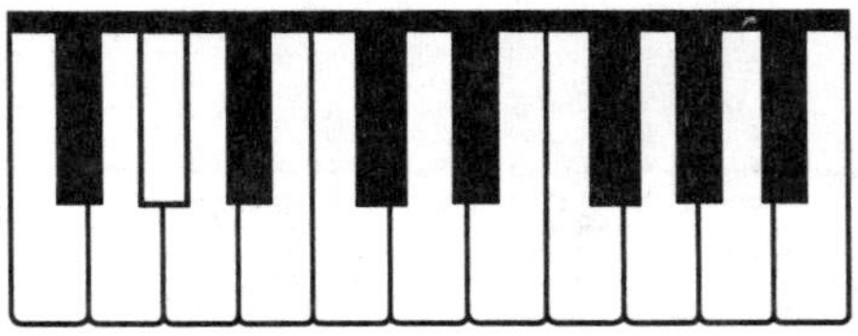 — L.H. 4 3 1 R.H. 1 2 4

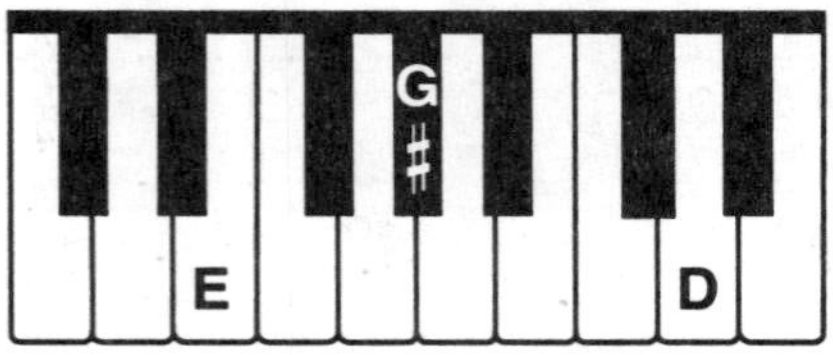

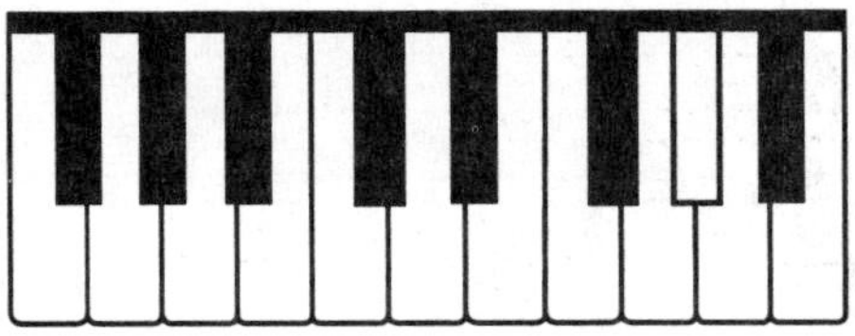

E G# D

V7 E7 (dominant 7th, 5th omitted)

3. Play each chord shown on the above keyboards in any convenient place on your piano, first with L.H., then with R.H. Use the fingering shown above each keyboard.

More Minors, Majors & Arpeggios

Assign with pages 38–39.

- Any MINOR TRIAD may be changed to a MAJOR TRIAD by RAISING the 3rd one half step!
- When the triad is in ROOT POSITION, you simply add an accidental before the MIDDLE NOTE to raise it one half step.

1. Change each of the following MINOR TRIADS to MAJOR TRIADS by adding an accidental before the MIDDLE NOTE to raise it one half step.
2. Write the name of each triad (after you have changed it) in the box below it.

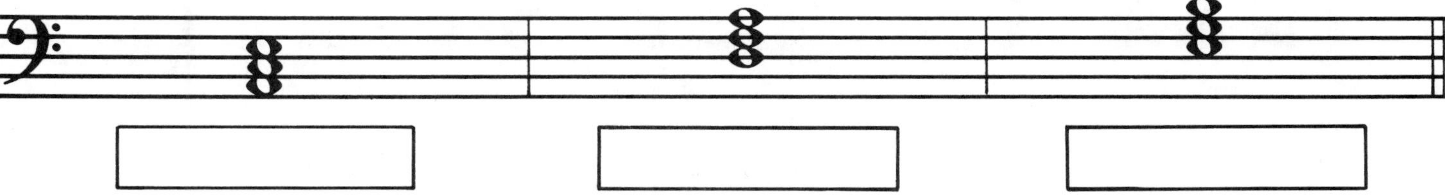

The only MAJOR TRIADS that have WHITE KEYS for the ROOT and FIFTH, and a BLACK KEY for the THIRD are the following:

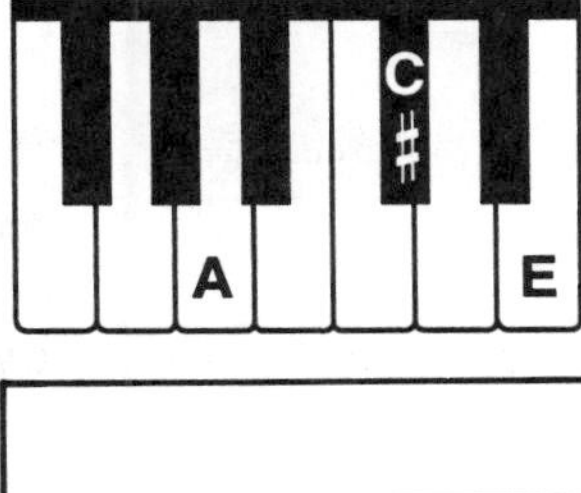

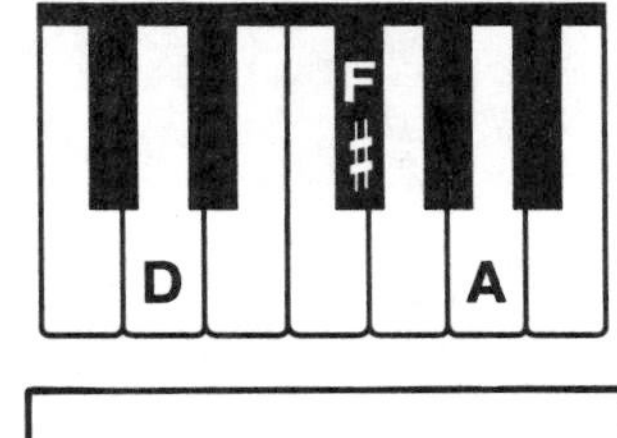

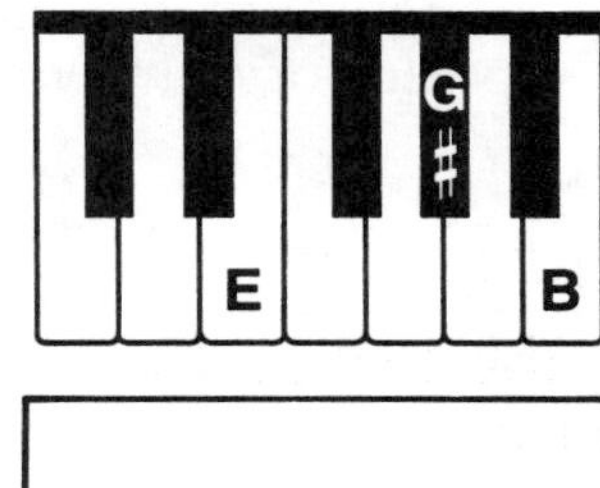

3. Write the name of each of the above triads in the box below it.

TWO OCTAVE ARPEGGIOS ON THE **A MAJOR, D MAJOR** & **E MAJOR** triads are fingered the same. Notice that with the R.H., the 2nd finger is used on the black keys; with L.H., the 3rd.

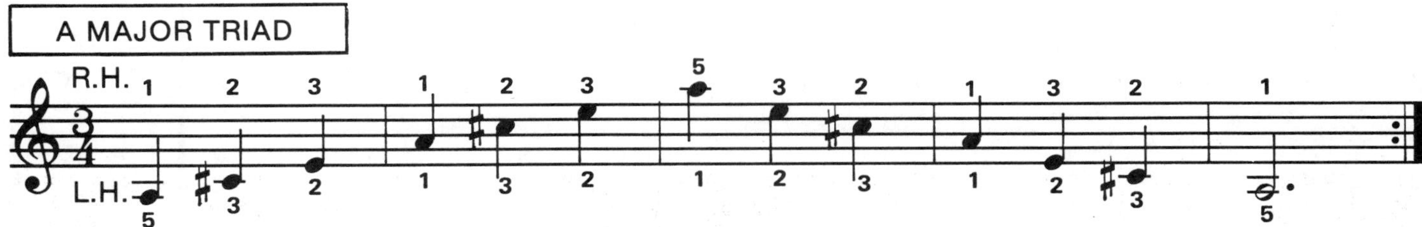

4. Write the name of the arpeggiated triad in the box at the beginning of each staff below.
5. Write the R.H. fingering ABOVE each note.
6. Write the L.H. fingering BELOW each note.
7. Play with R.H. as written.
8. Play with L.H. two octaves lower than written.

Assign with page 40.

The Key of F♯ Minor (Relative of A Major)

F♯ MINOR is the relative of **A MAJOR.**
Both keys have the same key signature (3 sharps, F♯, C♯, & G♯).

REMEMBER: The RELATIVE MINOR begins on the 6th tone of the MAJOR SCALE.

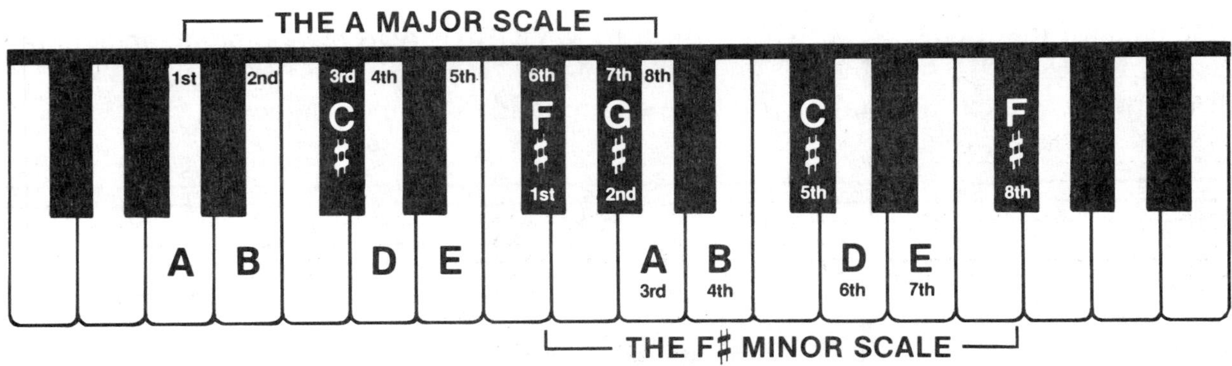

THE NATURAL MINOR SCALE. This scale uses *only* the tones of the relative major scale.

1. Play with hands separate.
2. (OPTIONAL) Play with hands together.

NOTE: Fingering in parentheses is optional, and should be used when continuing these scales upward or downward for two or more octaves.

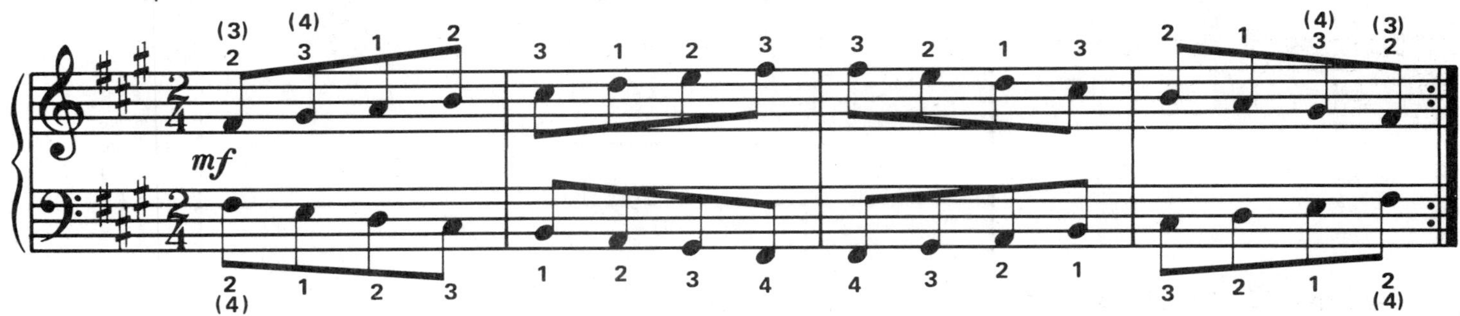

THE HARMONIC MINOR SCALE. The 7th tone (E) is raised one half step, ASCENDING & DESCENDING.

3. Add accidentals needed to change these NATURAL MINOR scales into HARMONIC MINOR scales.
4. Play with hands separate.
5. (OPTIONAL) Play with hands together.

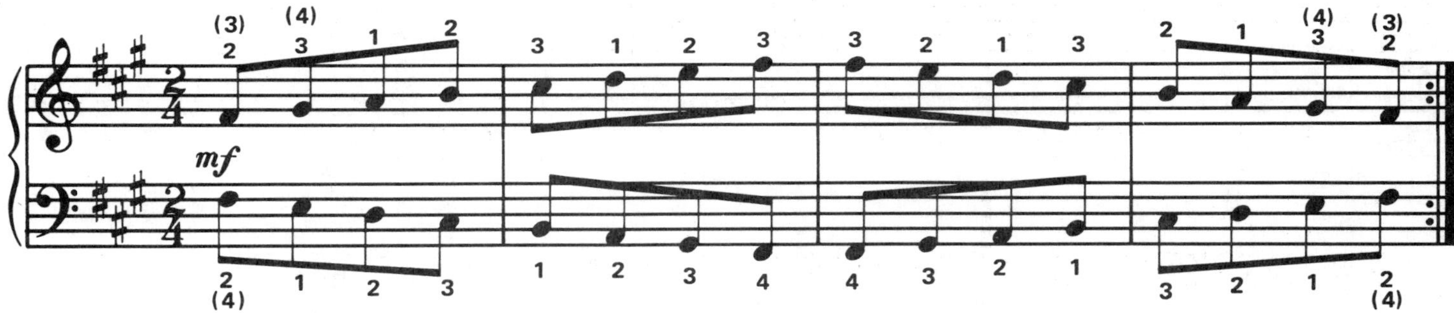

THE MELODIC MINOR SCALE. 6th (D) and 7th (E) raised one half step ASCENDING; DESCENDS like natural minor.

6. Add accidentals needed to change these NATURAL MINOR scales into MELODIC MINOR scales.
7. Play with hands separate.
8. (OPTIONAL) Play with hands together.

Note that the R.H. fingering for the MELODIC MINOR SCALE differs from the two other minor scales. It is played this way to avoid using the thumb on the raised 6th (D♯).

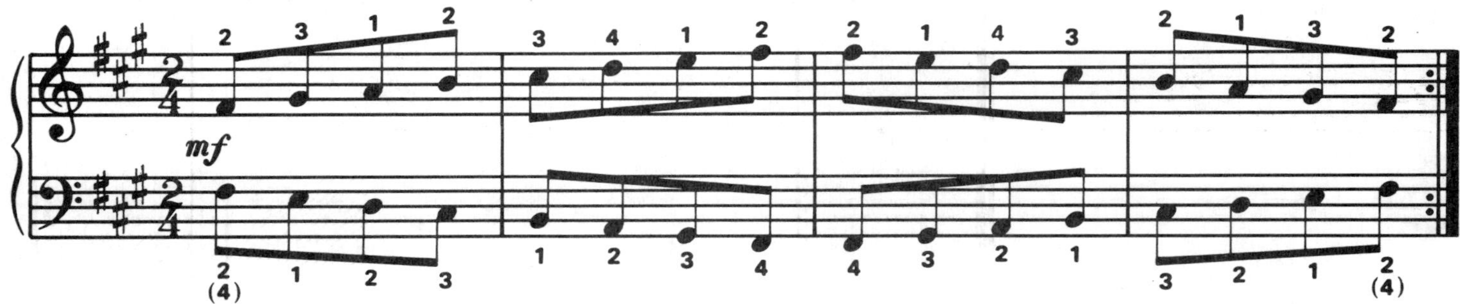

The Primary Chords in F♯ Minor

Assign with pages 40–42.

REMEMBER:
In MINOR KEYS: the **i chord** is the TONIC CHORD (minor).
the **iv chord** is the SUBDOMINANT CHORD (minor).
the **V7 chord** is the DOMINANT 7th CHORD.

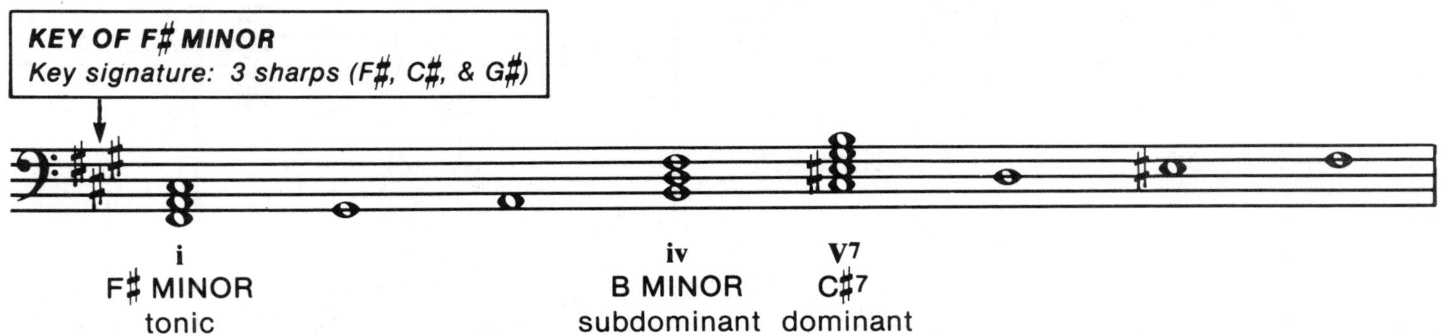

These positions are often used for smooth progressions:

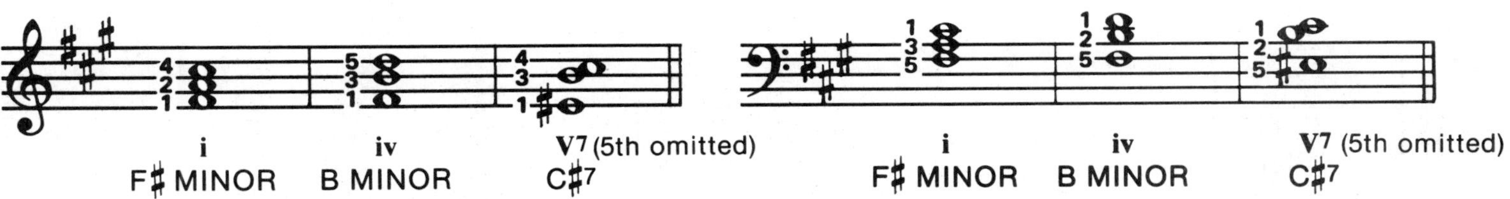

1. Add the F♯ MINOR key signature to each staff below.
2. Write the PRIMARY CHORDS in the KEY OF F♯ MINOR using the above positions.

3. Write the ROMAN NUMERALS (**i, iv,** or **V7**) in the boxes below.
4. Play.

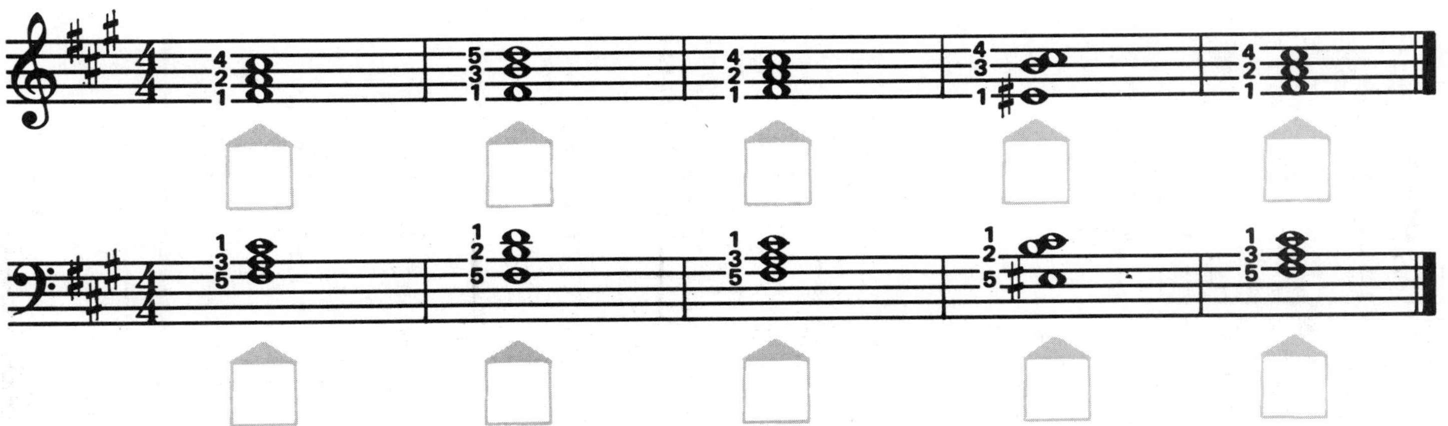

Assign with pages 40–42.

The Primary Chords in F♯ Minor—All Positions

1. In the blank measures after each ROOT POSITION chord, write the 2 INVERSIONS of the chord.

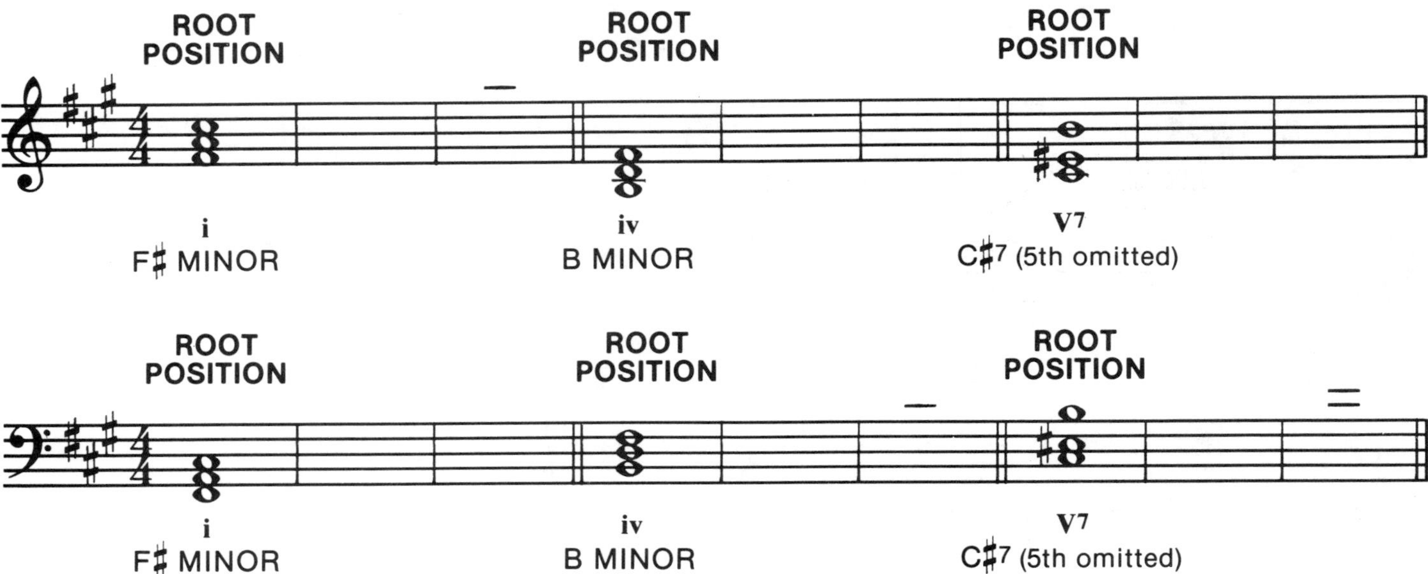

2. On the 2 keyboards to the right of each ROOT POSITION chord, write the letter names showing the 2 INVERSIONS of the chord.

ROOT POSITION — **INVERSIONS**

L.H. 5 3 1 R.H. 1 2 4 (F♯, A, C♯) | L.H. 5 3 1 R.H. 1 2 5 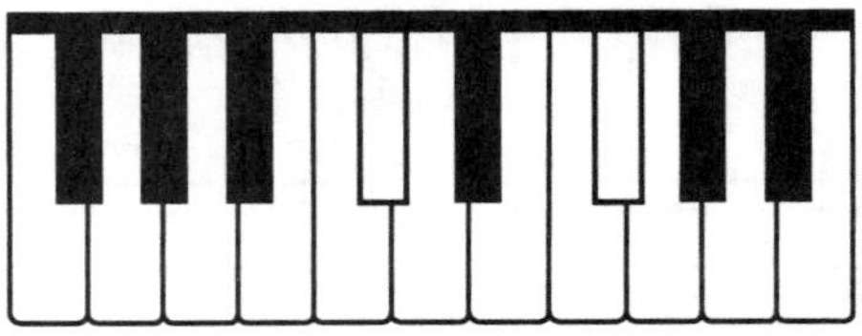 | L.H. 5 2 1 R.H. 1 3 5

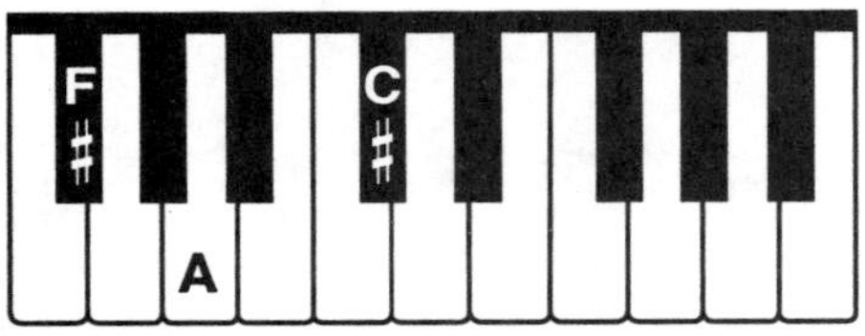

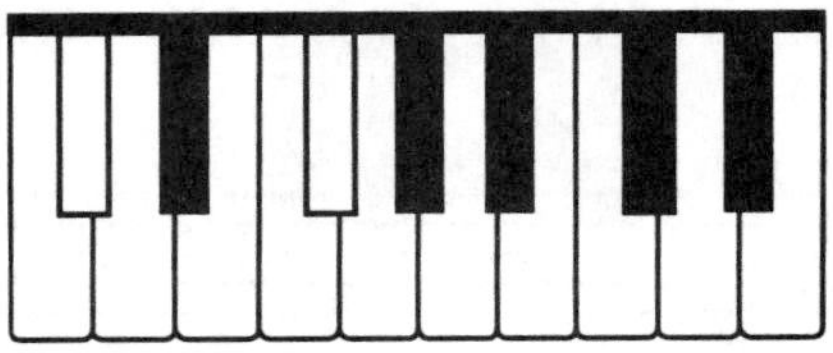

i F♯ MINOR (tonic)

L.H. 5 3 1 R.H. 1 2 4 (B, D, F♯) | L.H. 5 3 1 R.H. 1 2 5 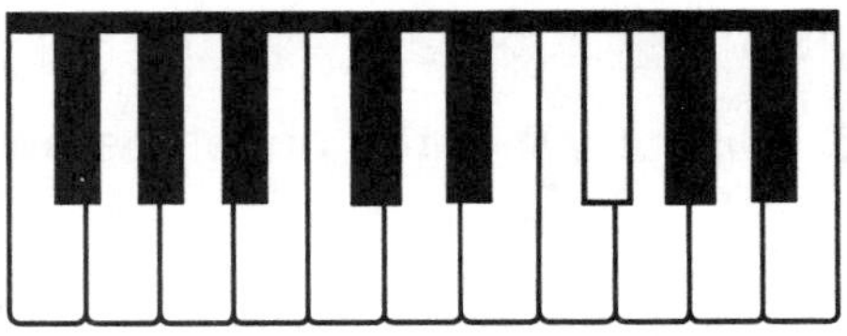 | L.H. 5 2 1 R.H. 1 3 5

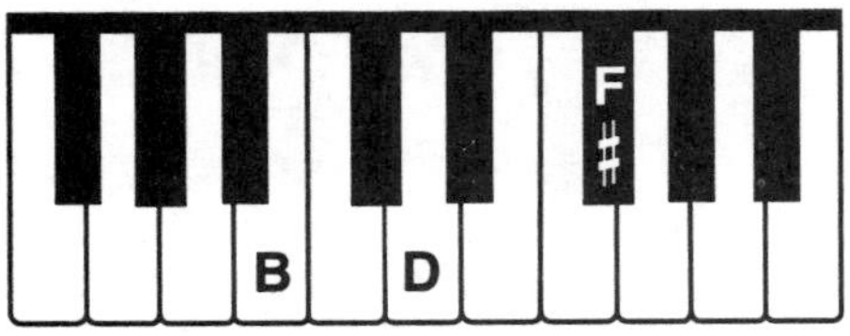

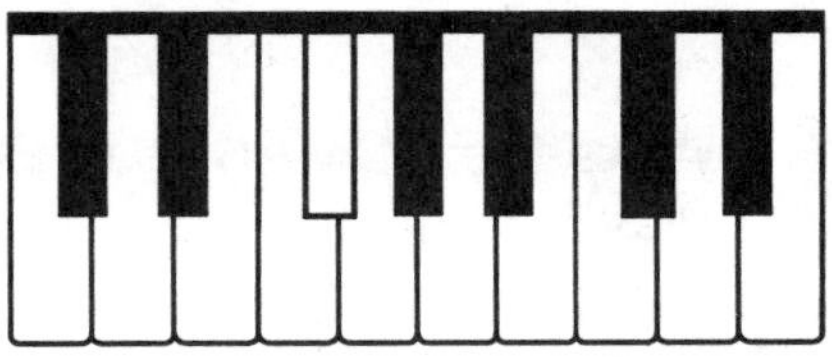

iv B MINOR (subdominant)

L.H. 5 3 1 R.H. 1 2 5 (C♯, E♯, B) | L.H. 5 2 1 R.H. 1 3 4 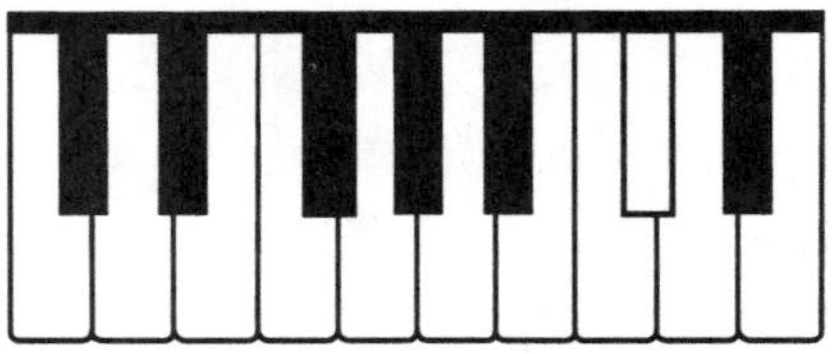 | L.H. 4 3 1 R.H. 1 2 4

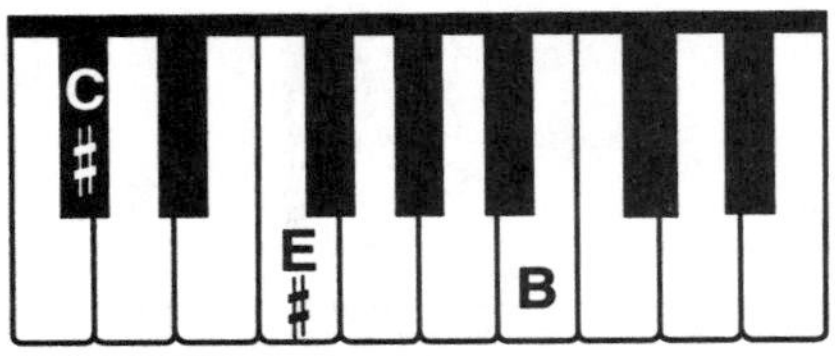

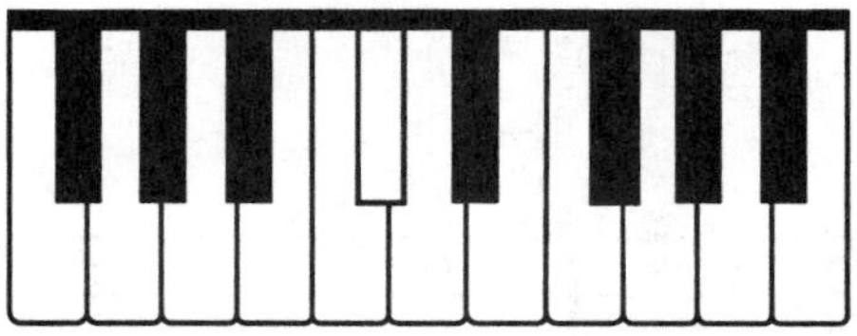

V7 C♯7 (dominant 7th, 5th omitted)

3. Play each chord shown on the above keyboards in any convenient place on your piano, first with L.H., then with R.H. Use the fingering shown above each keyboard.

Assign with page 43.

The E Major Scale

1. Write the letter names of the notes of the E MAJOR SCALE, from *left* to *right,* on the keyboard below. Be sure the WHOLE STEPS & HALF STEPS are correct!

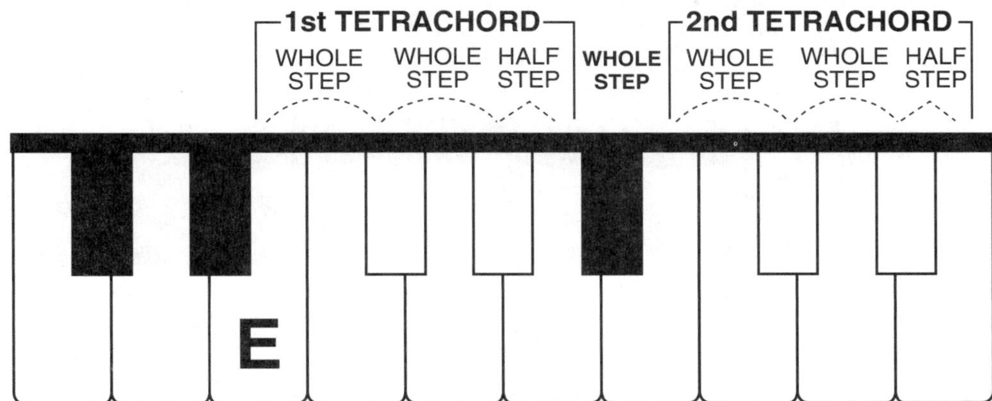

2. Check to be sure that you named the notes in the order of the musical alphabet. If you did, all the black keys will be named as *sharps,* not *flats.*

3. Complete the tetrachord beginning on E. Write one note over each finger number.

4. Complete the tetrachord beginning on B. Write one note over each finger number.

NOTE: The fingering for the E MAJOR SCALE is the same as for the C MAJOR, G MAJOR, D MAJOR & A MAJOR SCALES.

5. Write the fingering UNDER each note of the following LH scale. Cross 3 over 1 ascending. Pass 1 under 3 descending.

6. Play with LH.

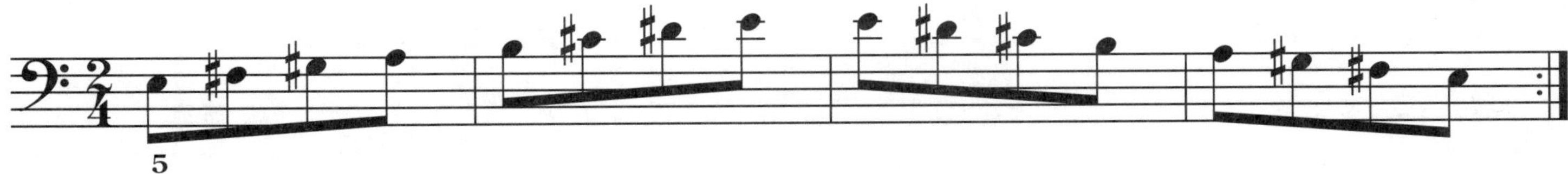

7. Write the fingering OVER each note of the following RH scale. Pass 1 under 3 ascending. Cross 3 over 1 descending.

8. Play with RH.

Assign with page 43.

Completing the Circle of 5ths:

The Sharp Key Signatures

Beginning with C and moving upward in 5ths CLOCKWISE, the order of keys around the circle is

C G D A E B F♯ C♯

Each key has one more sharp than the previous one, as you move around the circle clockwise.

The key of C MAJOR has NO SHARPS.

The key of G MAJOR has 1 SHARP (F♯).

The key of D MAJOR has 2 SHARPS (F♯ & C♯), etc., continuing around the circle until all the notes are sharp.

The key of C♯ MAJOR has 7 SHARPS: F♯, C♯, G♯, D♯, A♯, E♯, & B♯.

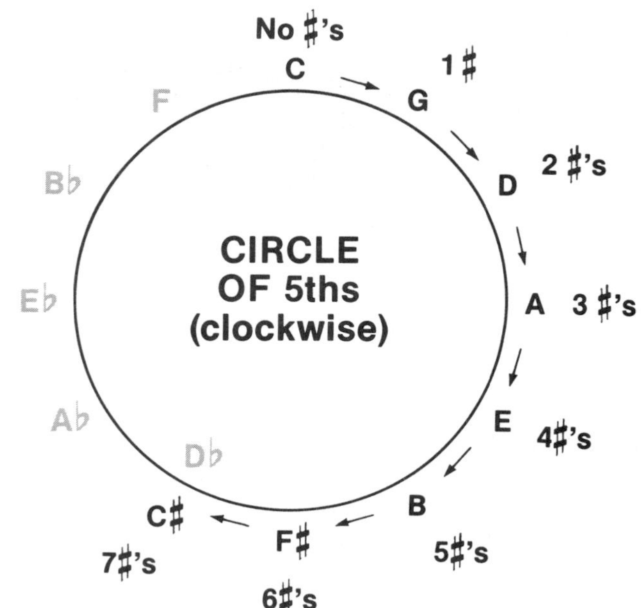

1. Copy the sharps of each key signature in the blank measure following it.

IMPORTANT!!

Notice that the sharps in the key signatures occur in the order of the letters (moving clockwise) around the Circle of 5ths, beginning with F.

F♯ C♯ G♯ D♯ A♯ E♯ B♯

The Primary Chords in E Major

Assign with pages 44–45.

REMEMBER: In MAJOR KEYS: the **I chord** is the TONIC CHORD (major).
the **IV chord** is the SUBDOMINANT CHORD (major).
the **V7 chord** is the DOMINANT 7th CHORD.

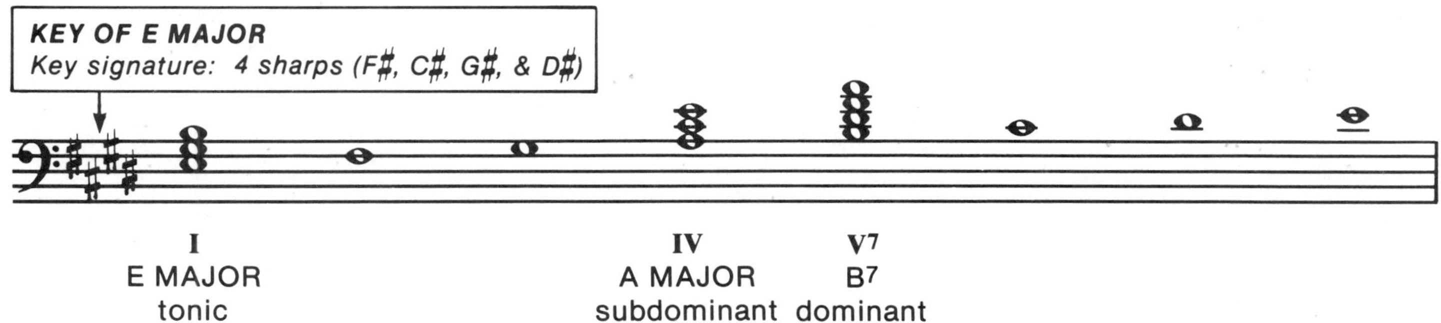

The following positions are often used for smooth progressions:

1. Add the E MAJOR key signature to each staff below.
2. Write the PRIMARY CHORDS in E MAJOR, using the above positions.

3. Write the ROMAN NUMERALS (**I, IV, V7**) in the boxes below.
4. Play.

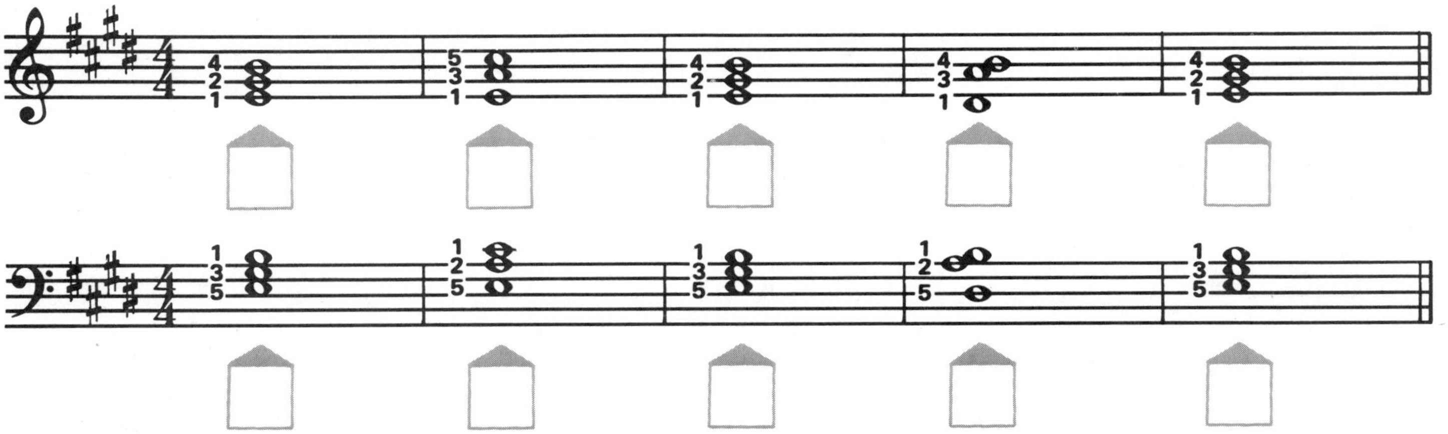

Assign with page 46.

The Primary Chords in E Major—All Positions

1. In the blank measures after each ROOT POSITION chord, write the 2 INVERSIONS of the chord.

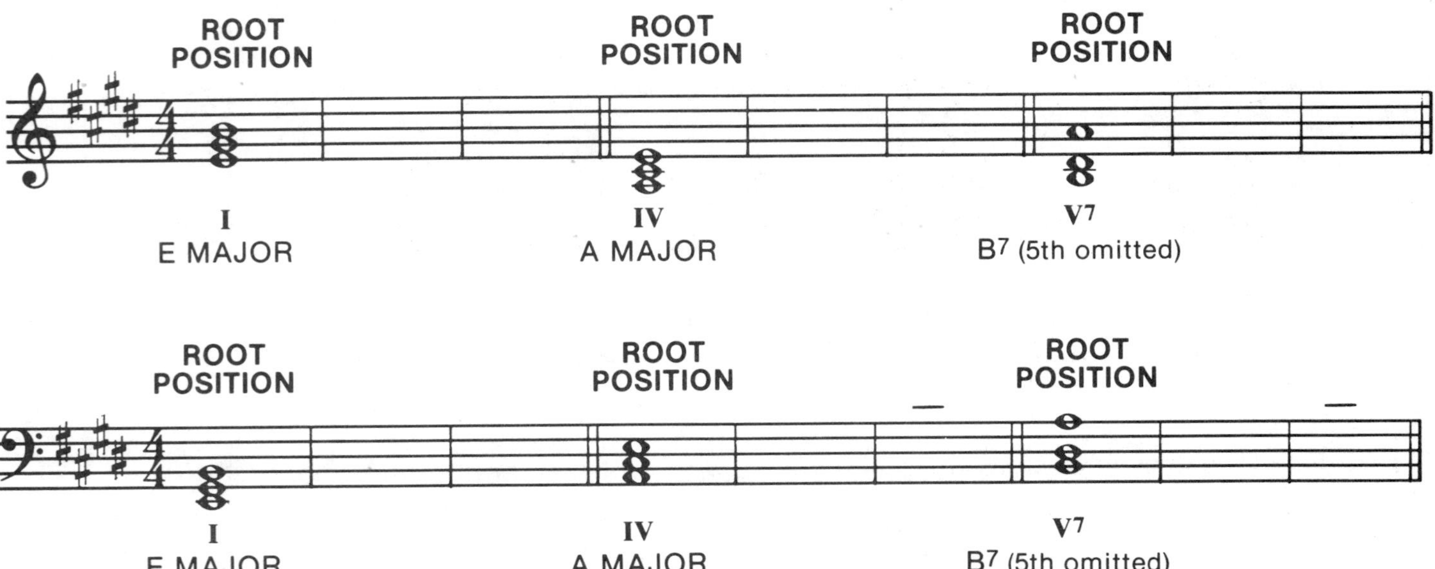

2. On the 2 keyboards to the right of each ROOT POSITION chord, write the letter names showing the 2 inversions of the chord.

ROOT POSITION | **INVERSIONS**

L.H. 5 2 1 R.H. 1 3 5 | L.H. 5 3 1 R.H. 1 2 5 | L.H. 5 2 1 R.H. 1 3 5

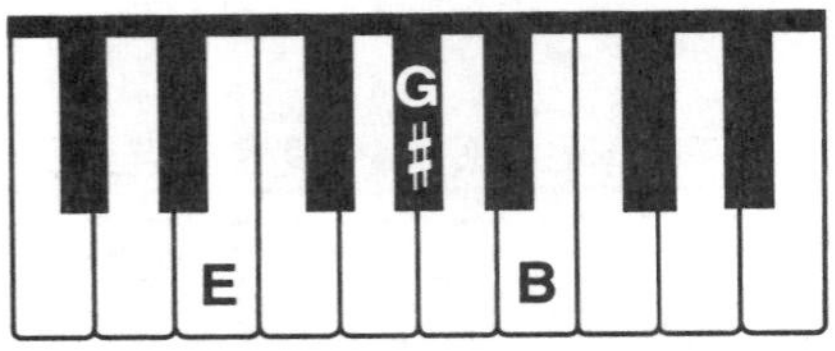

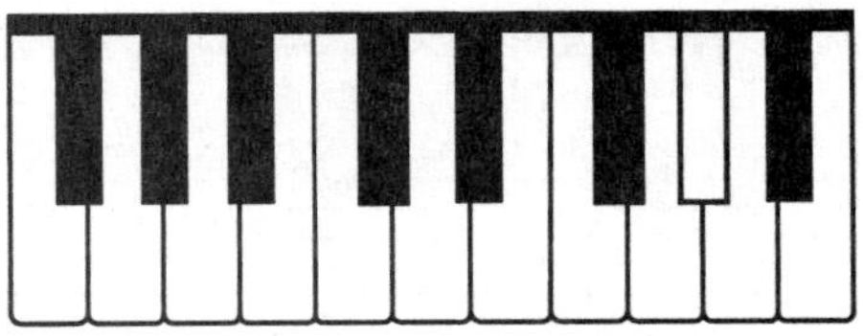

E G♯ B

I E MAJOR (tonic)

L.H. 5 2 1 R.H. 1 3 5 | L.H. 5 3 1 R.H. 1 2 5 | L.H. 5 2 1 R.H. 1 3 5

A C♯ E

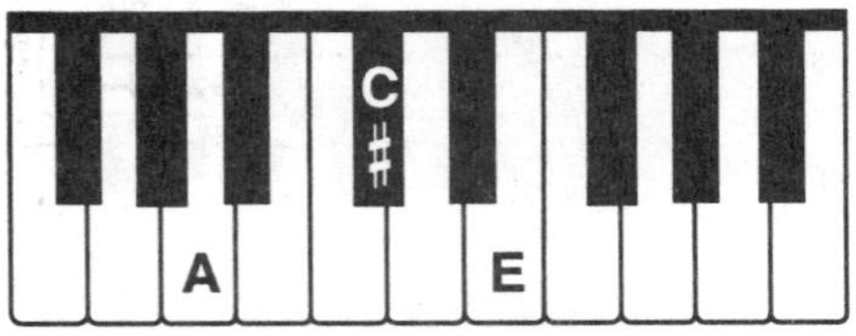

IV A MAJOR (subdominant)

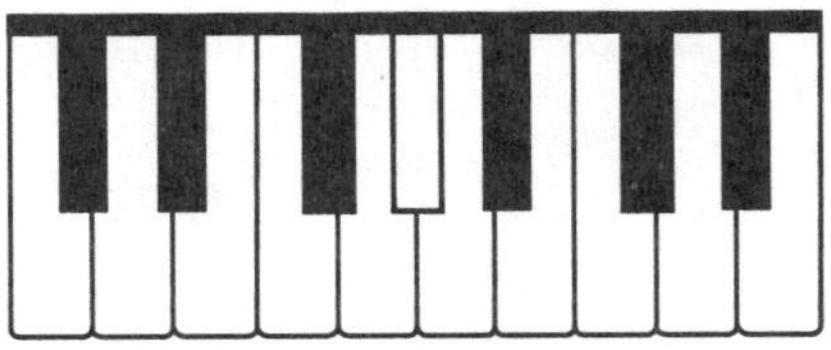

L.H. 5 3 1 R.H. 1 2 5 | L.H. 5 2 1 R.H. 1 3 4 | L.H. 4 3 1 R.H. 1 2 4

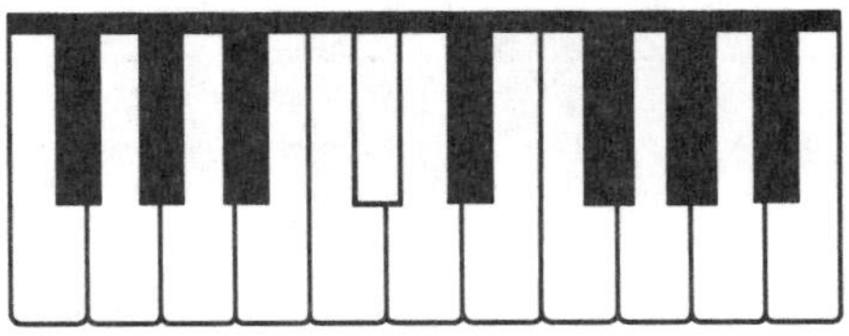

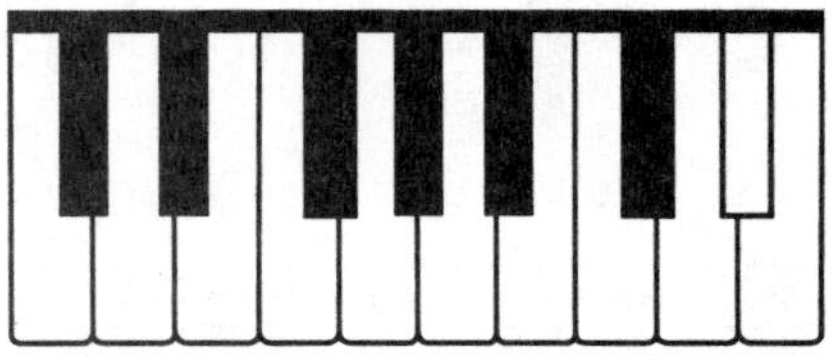

B D♯ A

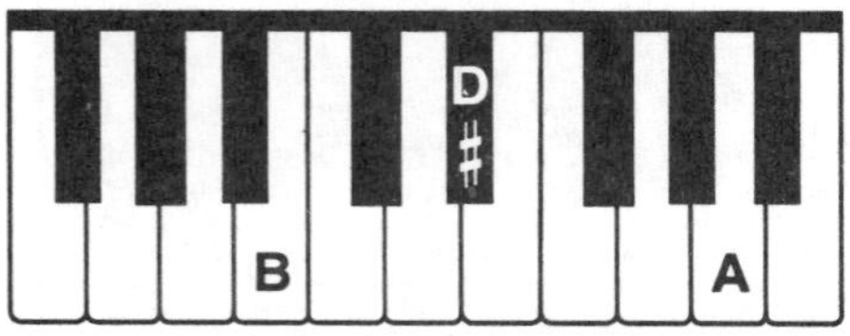

V7 B7 (dominant 7th, 5th omitted)

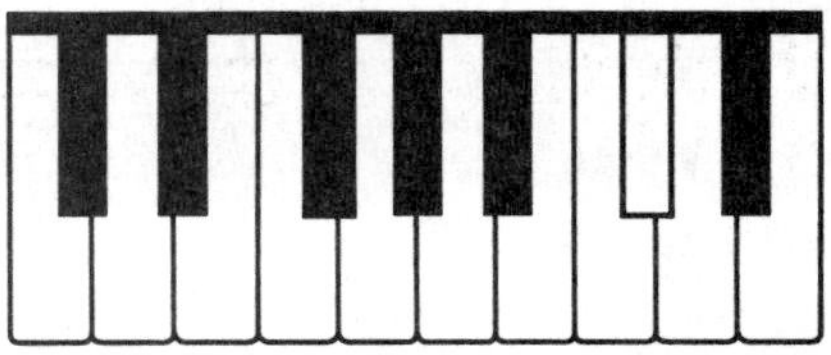

3. Play each chord shown on the above keyboards in any convenient place on your piano, first with L.H., then with R.H. Use the fingering shown above each keyboard.

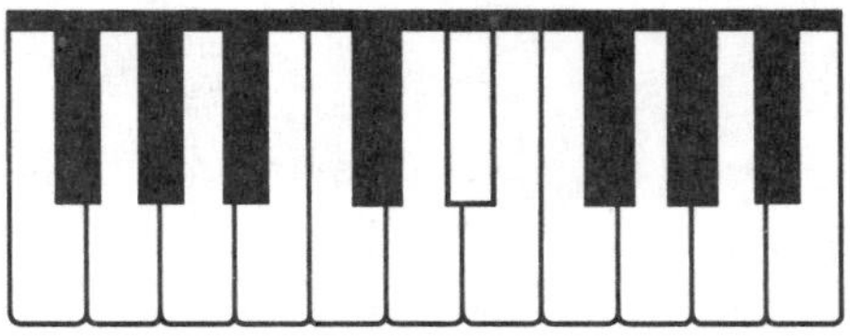

Assign with page 47.

The Key of C♯ Minor (Relative of E Major)

C♯ MINOR is the relative of **E MAJOR.**

Both keys have the same key signature (4 sharps, F♯, C♯, G♯, & D♯).

REMEMBER: The RELATIVE MINOR begins on the 6th tone of the MAJOR SCALE.

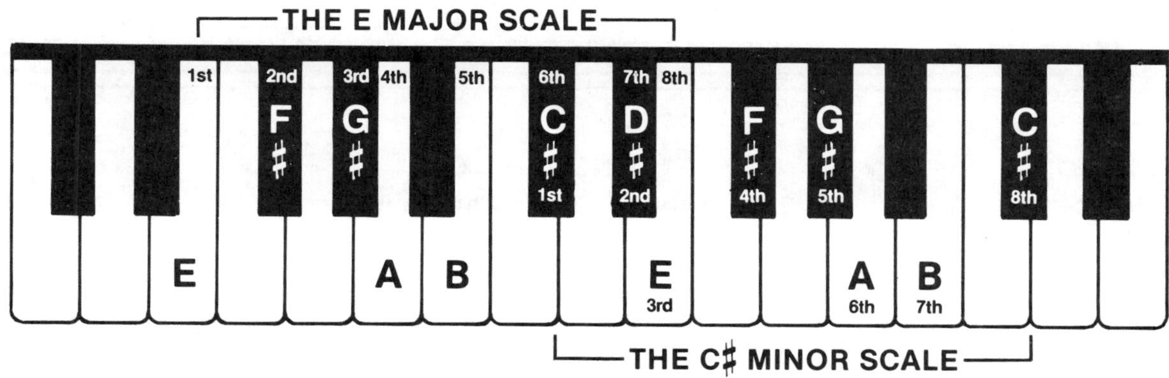

THE NATURAL MINOR SCALE. This scale uses *only* the tones of the relative major scale.

1. Play with hands separate, then together. The fingering in parentheses is for 2 or more octaves.

THE HARMONIC MINOR SCALE. The 7th tone (B) is raised 1 half step (to B♯), ASCENDING & DESCENDING.

2. Add accidentals needed to change these NATURAL MINOR scales into HARMONIC MINOR SCALES.
3. Play with hands separate, then together.

THE MELODIC MINOR SCALE. 6th (A) & 7th (B) raised 1 half step (to A♯ & B♯) ASCENDING; DESCENDS like natural minor.

4. Add accidentals needed to change these NATURAL MINOR scales into MELODIC MINOR scales.
5. Play with hands separate.
6. (OPTIONAL) Play with hands together.

Note that the R.H. fingering for the MELODIC MINOR scale differs from the two other minor scales. This avoids using the thumb on the raised 6th (A♯).

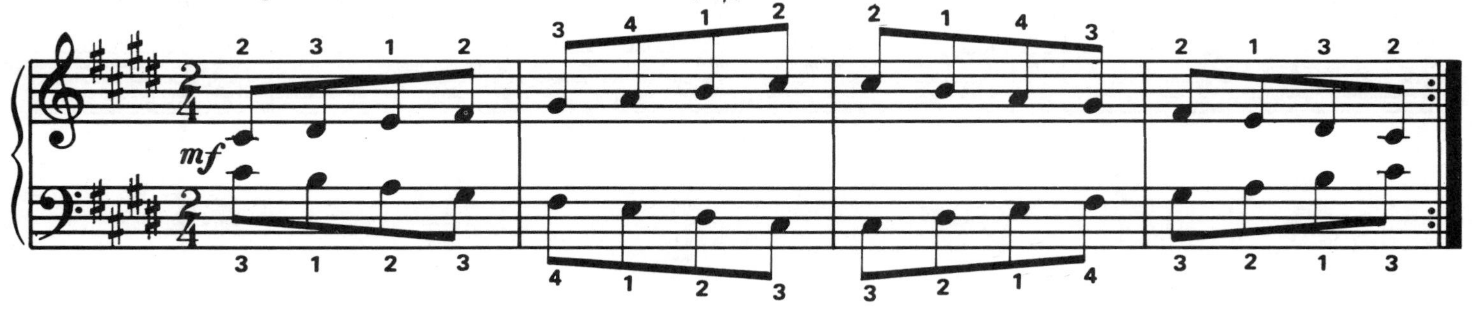

Assign with page 47.

The Primary Chords in C♯ Minor

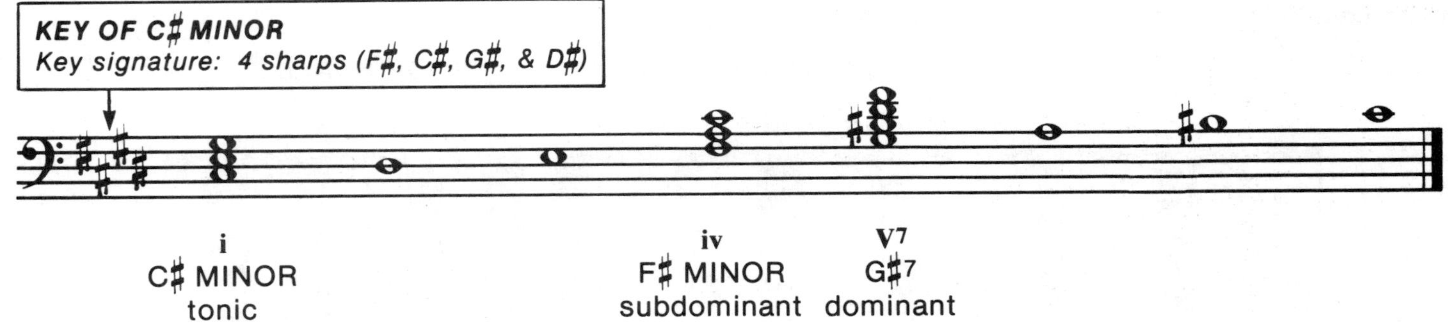

These positions are often used for smooth progressions:

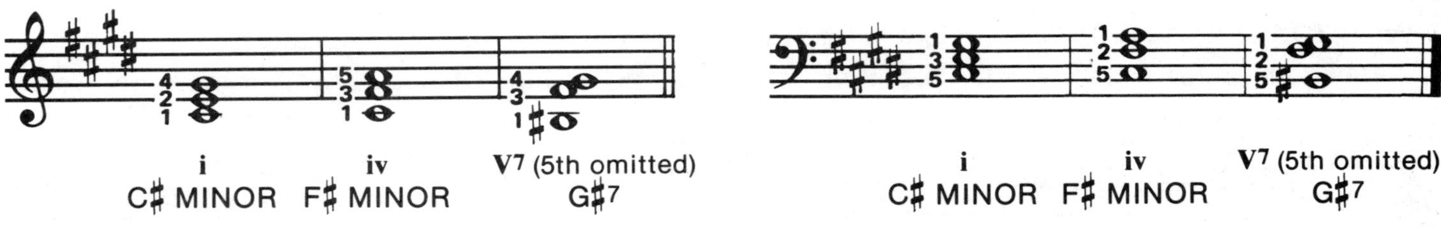

1. Add the C♯ MINOR key signature to each staff below.
2. Write the PRIMARY CHORDS in the KEY OF C♯ MINOR using the above positions.

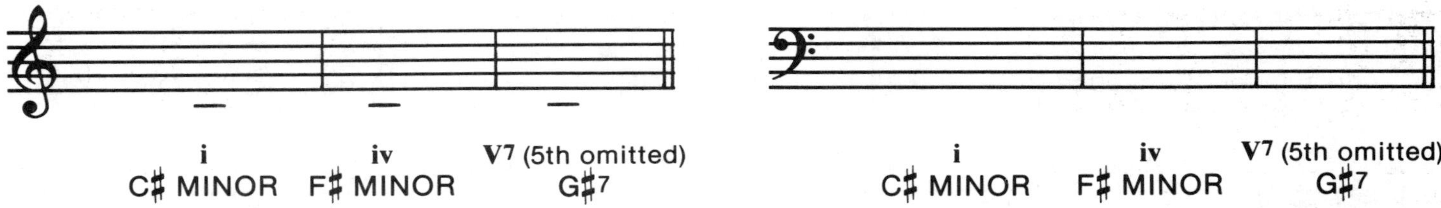

3. Write the ROMAN NUMERALS (**i**, **iv**, or **V7**) in the boxes below.
4. Play.

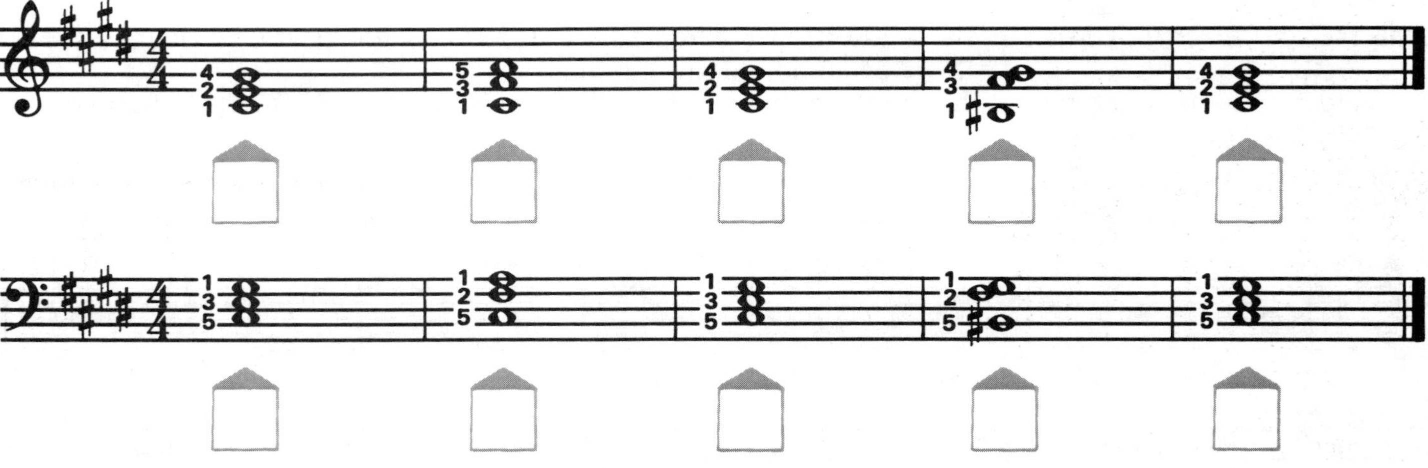

Assign with pages 48–49.

The Primary Chords in C♯ Minor—All Positions

1. In the blank measures after each ROOT POSITION chord, write the 2 INVERSIONS of the chord.

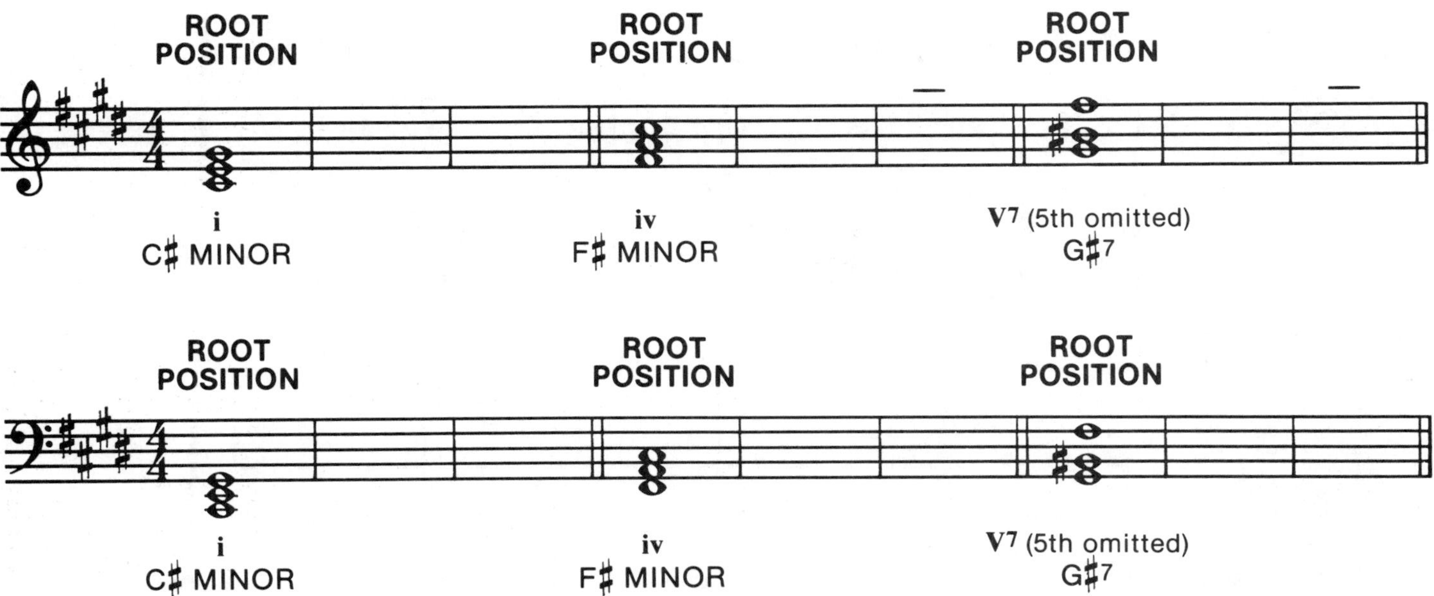

2. On the 2 keyboards to the right of each ROOT POSITION chord, write the letter names showing the 2 INVERSIONS of the chord.

ROOT POSITION — **INVERSIONS**

L.H. 5 3 1 R.H. 1 2 4 — L.H. 5 3 1 R.H. 1 2 5 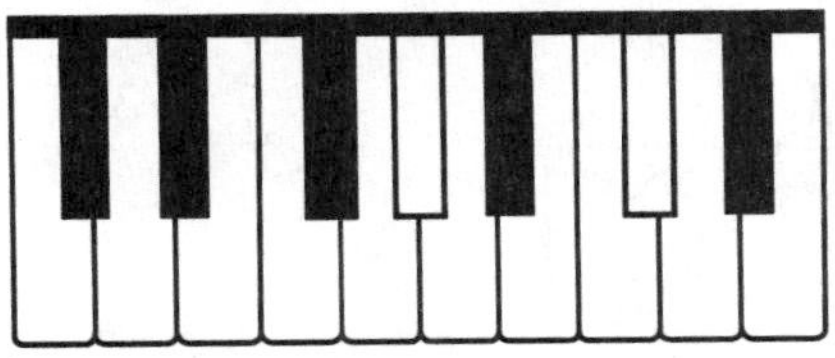 — L.H. 5 2 1 R.H. 1 3 5

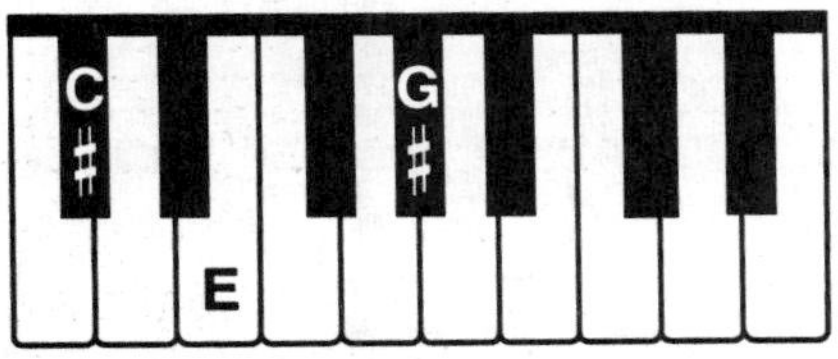

C♯ E G♯

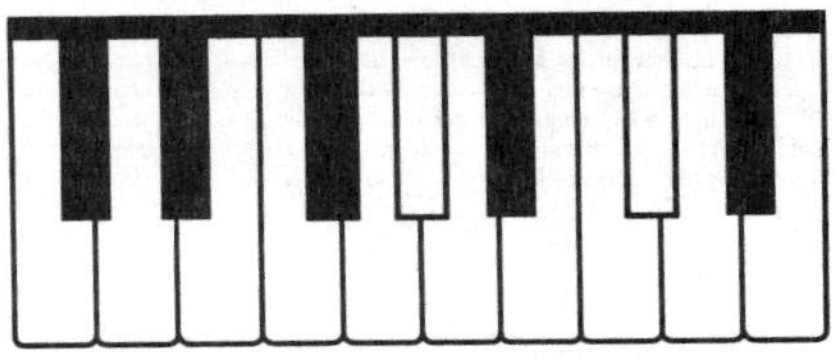

i C♯ MINOR (tonic)

L.H. 5 3 1 R.H. 1 2 4 — L.H. 5 3 1 R.H. 1 2 5 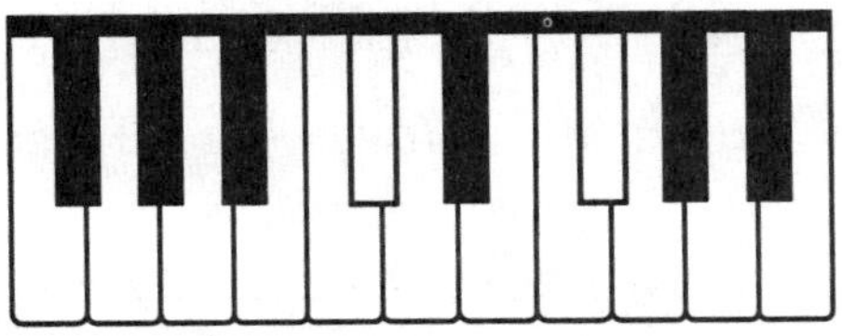 — L.H. 5 2 1 R.H. 1 3 5

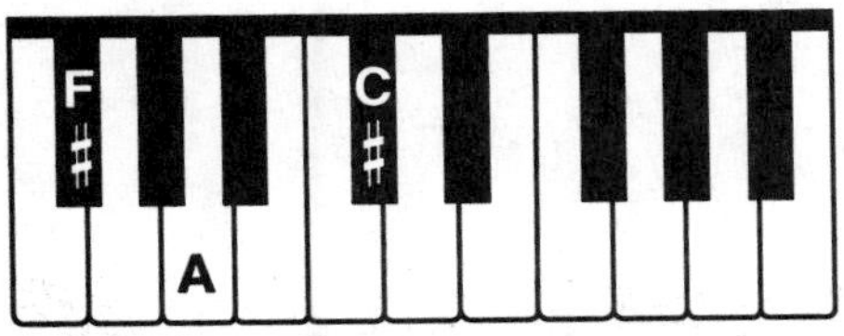

F♯ A C♯

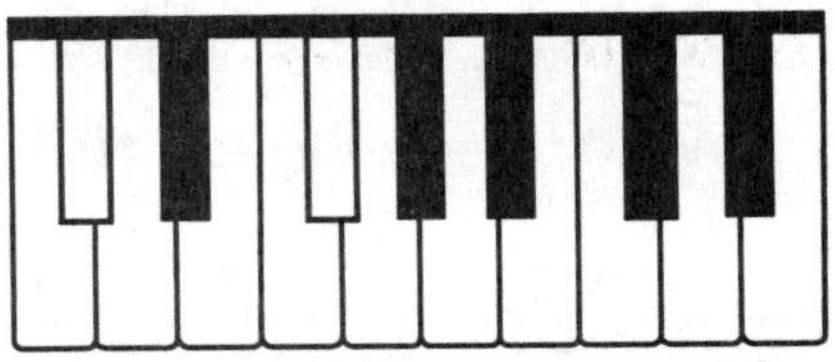

iv F♯ MINOR (subdominant)

L.H. 5 3 1 R.H. 1 2 5 — L.H. 5 2 1 R.H. 1 3 4 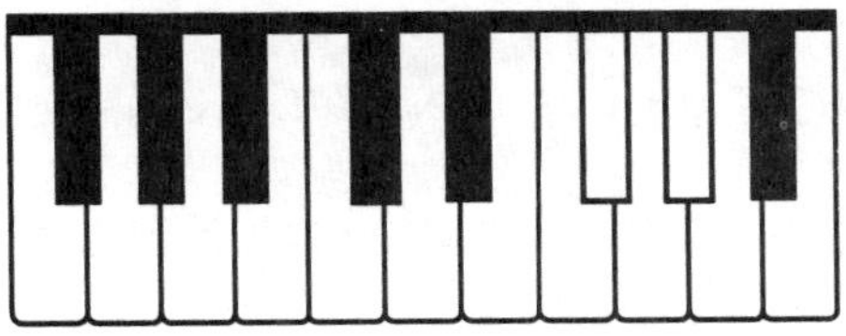 — L.H. 4 3 1 R.H. 1 2 4

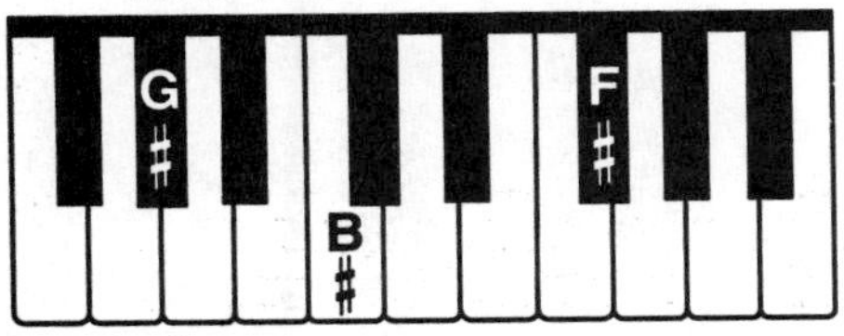

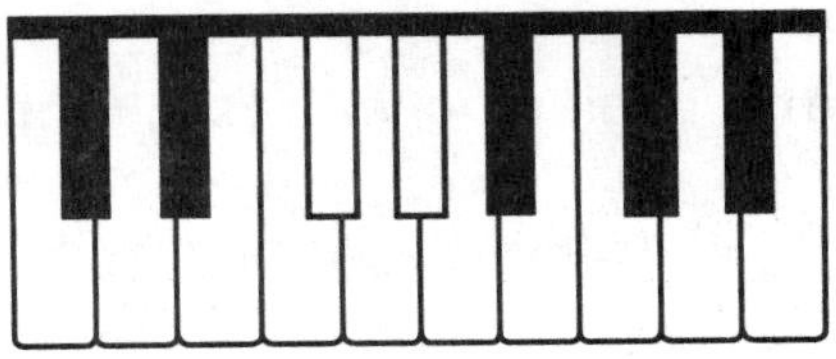

G♯ B♯ F♯

V7 G♯7 (dominant 7th, 5th omitted)

3. Play each chord shown on the above keyboards in any convenient place on your piano, first with L.H., then with R.H. Use the fingering shown above each keyboard.

Assign with page 50.

The E♭ Major Scale

1. Write the letter names of the notes of the E♭ MAJOR SCALE, from *left to right,* on the keyboard below. Be sure the WHOLE STEPS & HALF STEPS are correct!

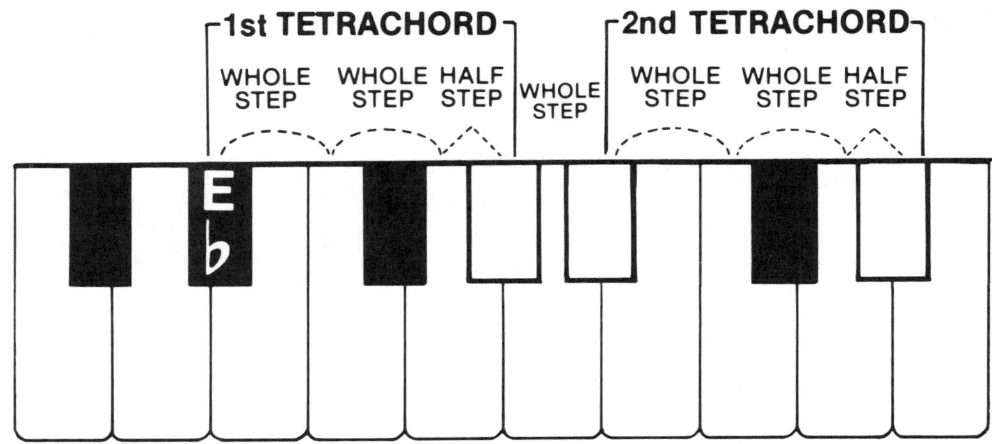

2. Check to be sure that you wrote A♭ as the 4th note of the scale, and B♭ as the 5th note. These notes cannot be called G♯ and A♯, because scale notes must always be named in alphabetical order. (You cannot have two G's and no A's, or two A's and no B's!)

3. Complete the tetrachord beginning on E♭. Write one note over each finger number.

4. Complete the tetrachord beginning on B♭. Write one note over each finger number.

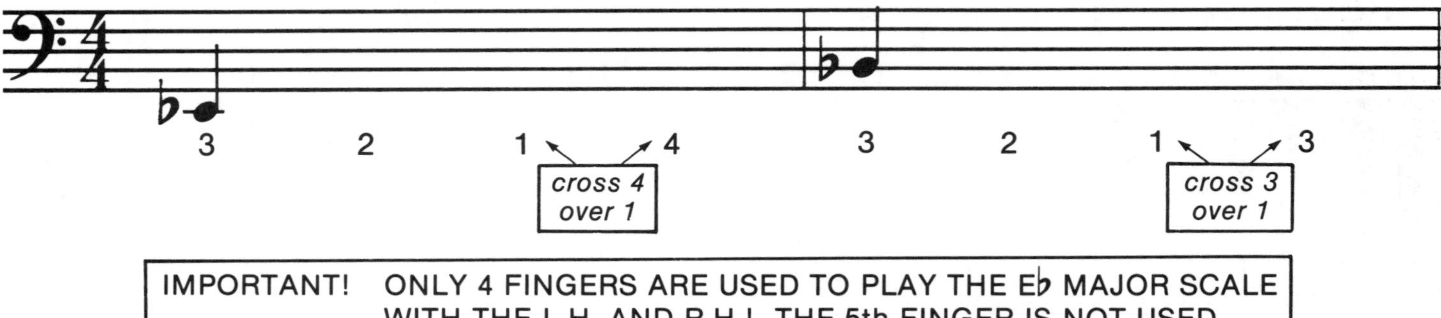

IMPORTANT! ONLY 4 FINGERS ARE USED TO PLAY THE E♭ MAJOR SCALE WITH THE L.H. AND R.H.! THE 5th FINGER IS NOT USED.

Beginning with L.H. 3, the scale is fingered in groups of 3 2 1 - 4 3 2 1; end on 3.

5. Write the fingering UNDER each note of the following L.H. scale. 6. Play with L.H.

After beginning with R.H. 3, the finger groups then fall 1 2 3 4 - 1 2 3.

7. Write the fingering OVER each note of the following R.H. scale. 8. Play with R.H.

3

The Primary Chords in E♭ Major

Assign with pages 50–51.

KEY OF E♭ MAJOR
Key Signature: 3 flats (B♭, E♭, & A♭)

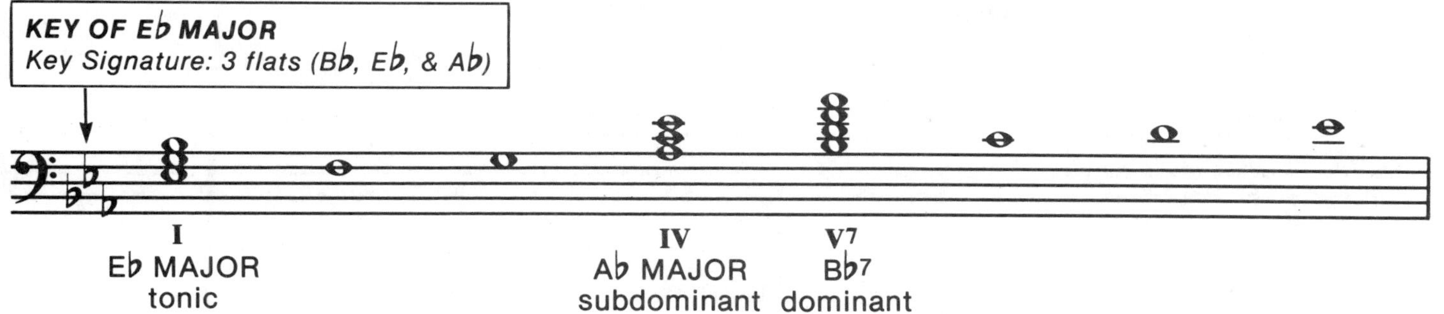

The following positions are often used for smooth progressions:

1. Add the E♭ MAJOR key signature to each staff below.
2. Write the PRIMARY CHORDS in E♭ MAJOR, using the above positions.

3. Write the ROMAN NUMERALS (**I, IV, V7**) in the boxes below.
4. Play.

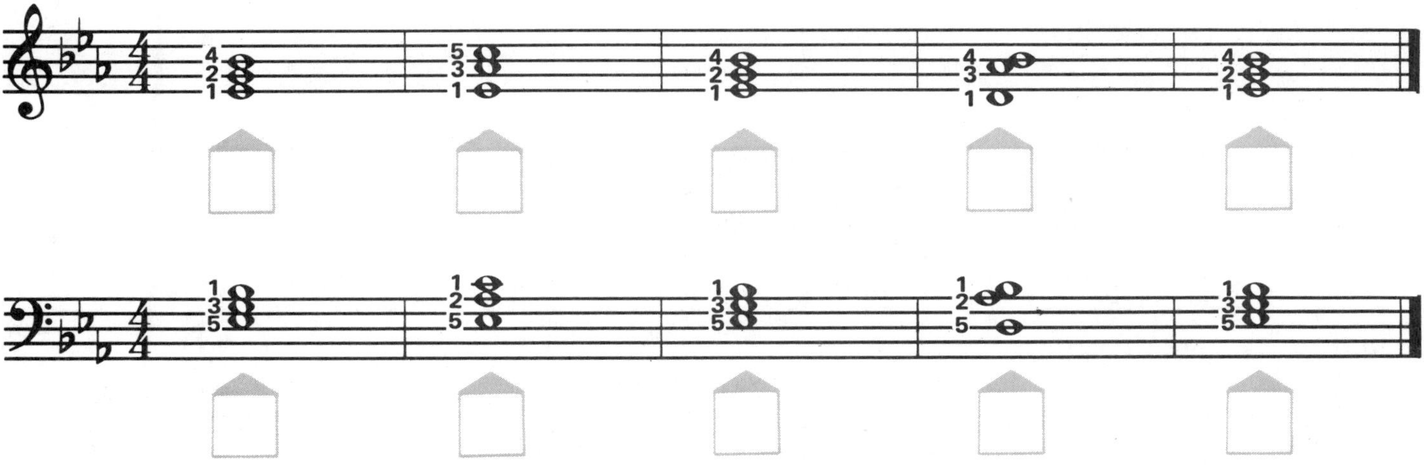

Assign with pages 52–53.

The Primary Chords in E♭ Major—All Positions

1. In the blank measures after each ROOT POSITION chord, write the 2 INVERSIONS of the chord.

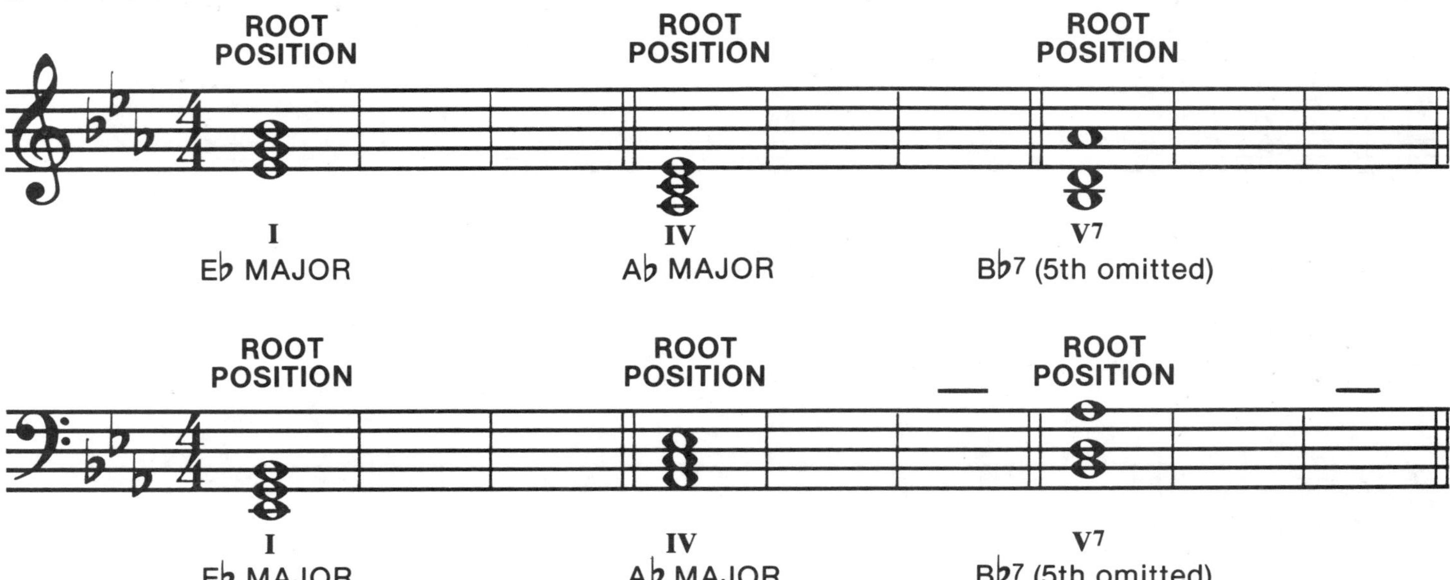

2. On the 2 keyboards to the right of each ROOT POSITION chord, write the letter names showing the 2 inversions of the chord.

ROOT POSITION — **INVERSIONS**

L.H. 5 3 1 R.H. 1 2 4 — L.H. 5 3 1 R.H. 1 2 5 — L.H. 5 2 1 R.H. 1 3 5

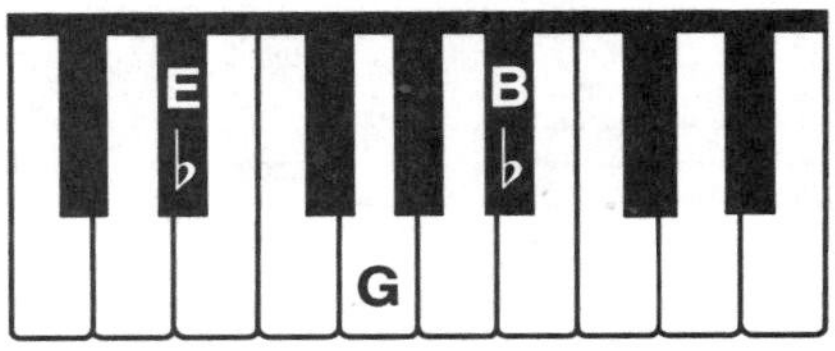

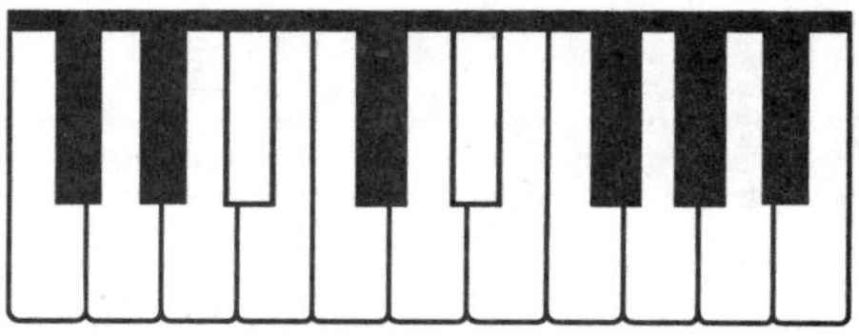

E♭ B♭ G

I E♭ MAJOR (tonic)

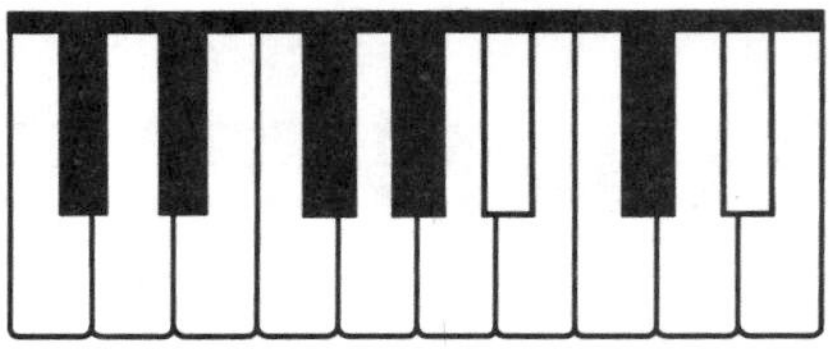

L.H. 5 3 1 R.H. 1 2 4 — L.H. 5 3 1 R.H. 1 2 5 — L.H. 5 2 1 R.H. 1 3 5

A♭ E♭ C

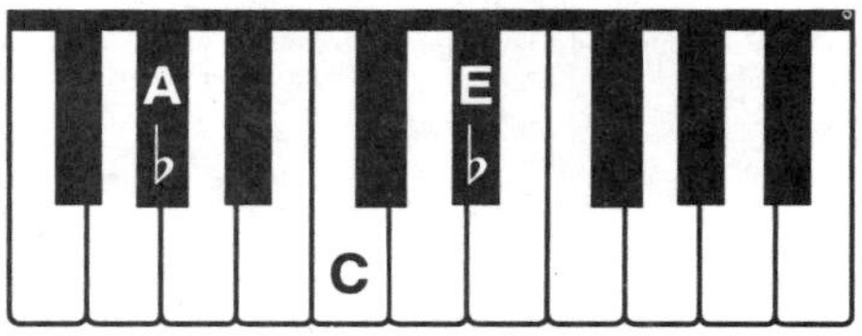

IV A♭ MAJOR (subdominant)

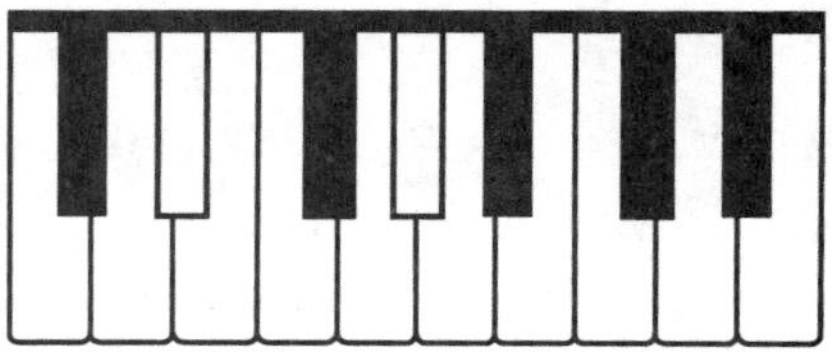

L.H. 5 3 1 R.H. 1 2 5 — L.H. 5 2 1 R.H. 1 3 4 — L.H. 4 3 1 R.H. 1 2 4

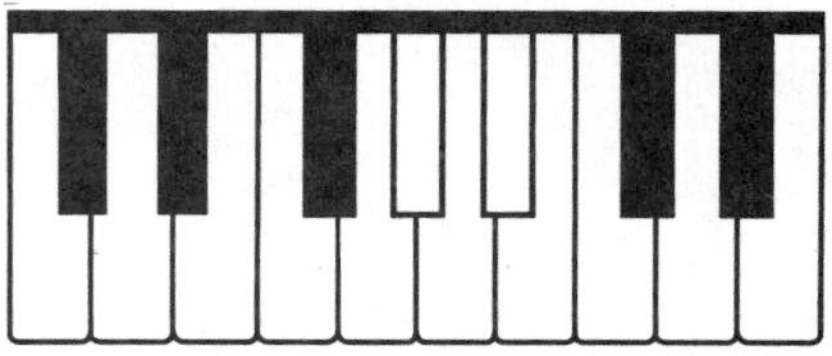

B♭ A♭ D

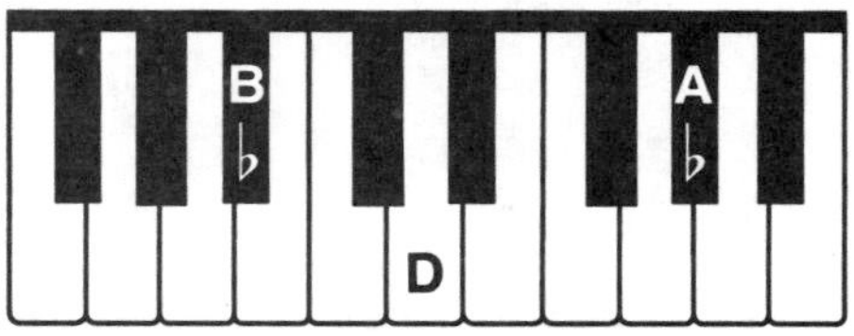

V7 B♭7 (dominant 7th, 5th omitted)

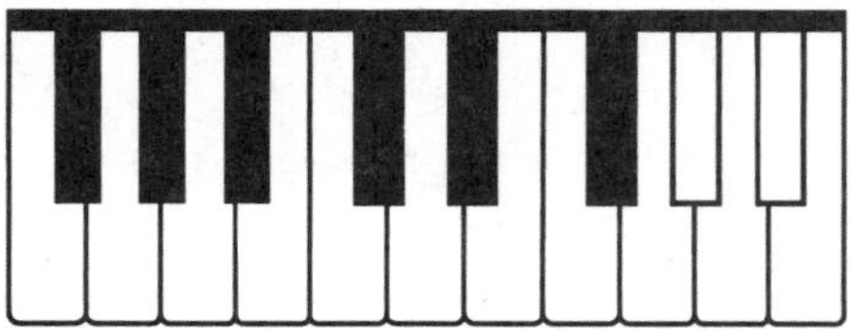

3. Play each chord shown on the above keyboards in any convenient place on your piano, first with L.H., then with R.H. Use the fingering shown above each keyboard.

Assign with page 54.

The Key of C Minor (Relative of E♭ Major)

C MINOR is the relative of **E♭ MAJOR.**
Both keys have the same key signature (**3** flats, B♭, E♭, & A♭).
REMEMBER: The RELATIVE MINOR begins on the 6th tone of the MAJOR SCALE.

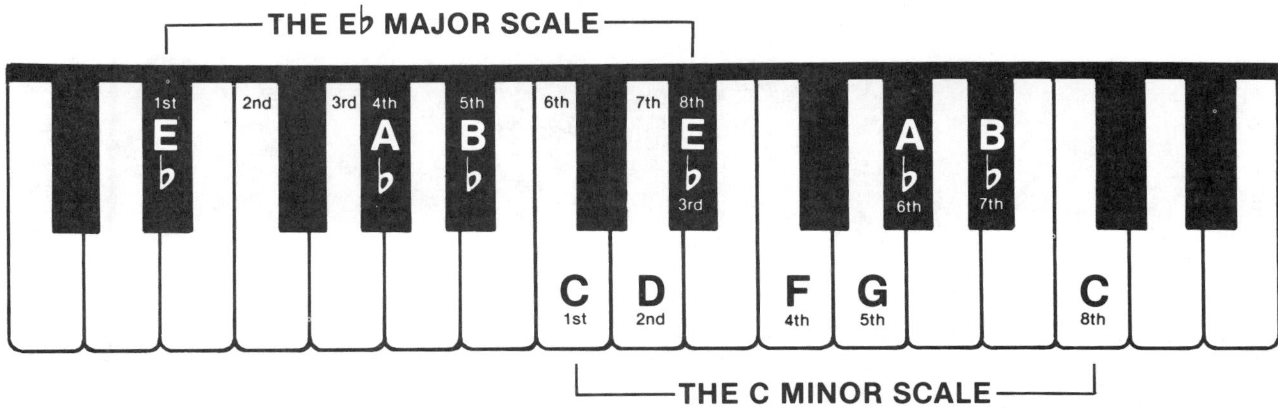

THE NATURAL MINOR SCALE. This scale uses *only* the tones of the relative major scale.

1. Play with hands separate, then together.

THE HARMONIC MINOR SCALE. The 7th tone (B♭) is raised one half step (to B♮), ASCENDING & DESCENDING.

2. Add accidentals needed to change these NATURAL MINOR scales into HARMONIC MINOR scales.
3. Play with hands separate, then together.

THE MELODIC MINOR SCALE. 6th (A♭) & 7th (B♭) raised one half step (to A♮ & B♮) ASCENDING; descends like natural minor.

4. Add accidentals needed to change these NATURAL MINOR scales into MELODIC MINOR scales.
5. Play with hands separate. 6. (OPTIONAL) Play with hands together.

The Primary Chords in C Minor

Assign with pages 54–55.

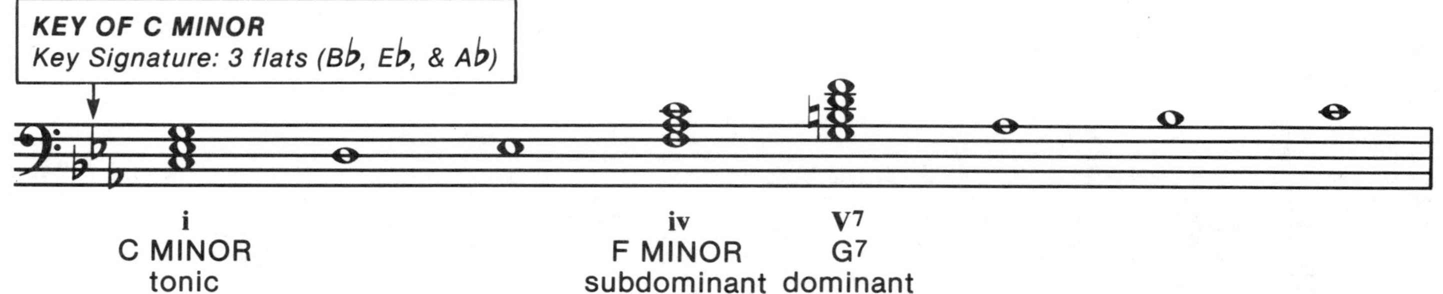

These positions are often used for smooth progressions:

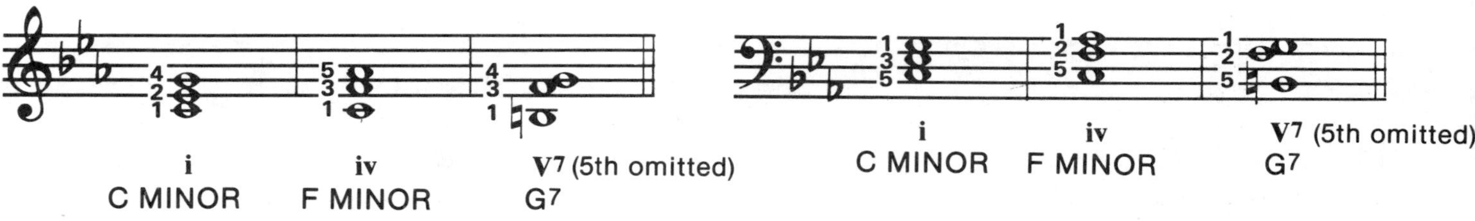

1. Add the C MINOR key signature to each staff below.
2. Write the PRIMARY CHORDS in the KEY OF C MINOR using the above positions.

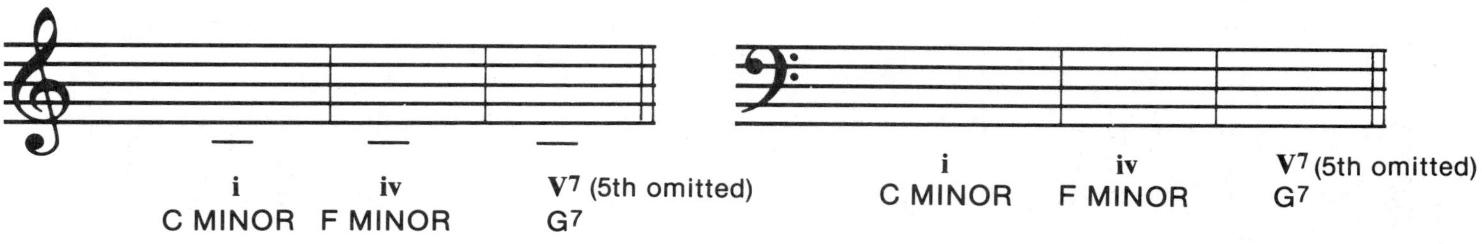

3. Write the ROMAN NUMERALS (**i**, **iv**, or **V7**) in the boxes below.
4. Play.

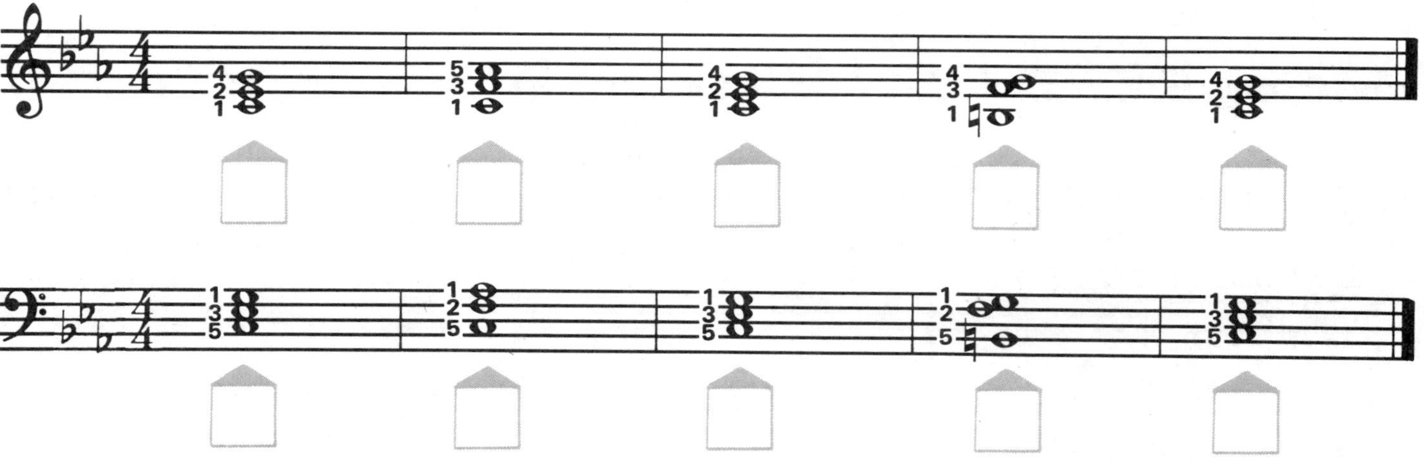

Assign with pages 54–55.

The Primary Chords in C Minor—All Positions

1. In the blank measures after each ROOT POSITION chord, write the 2 INVERSIONS of the chord.

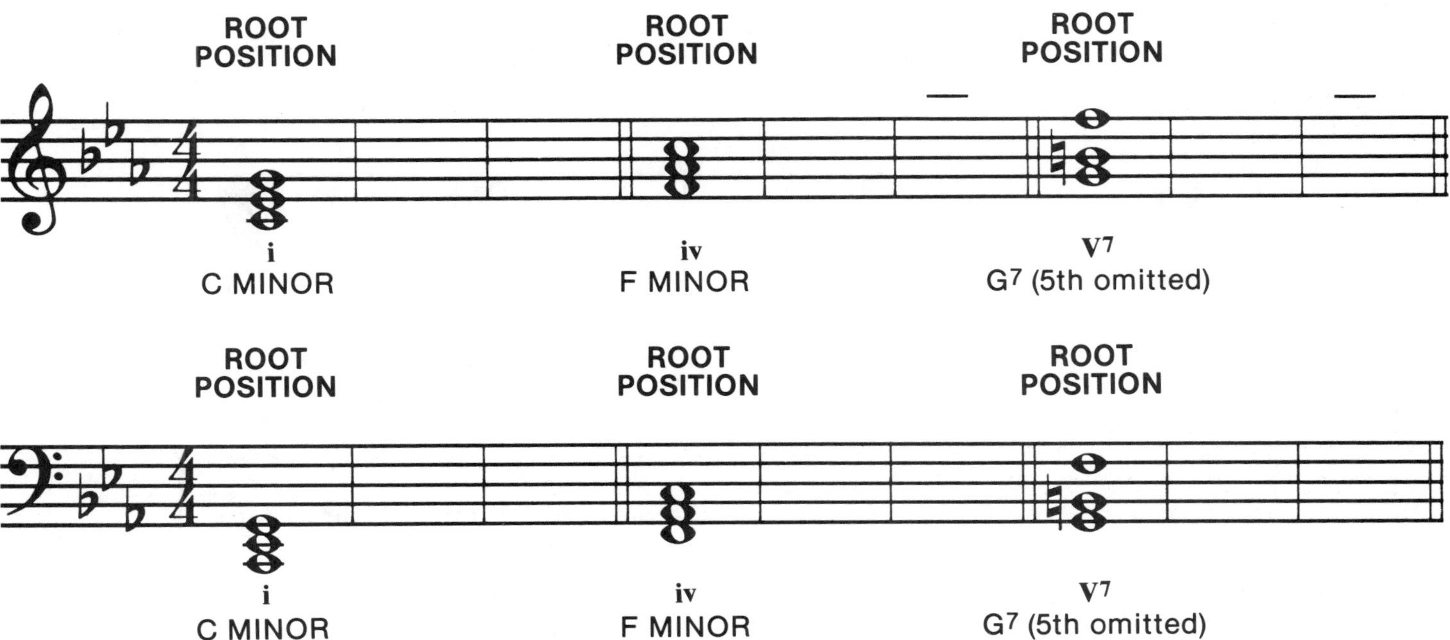

2. On the 2 keyboards to the right of each ROOT POSITION chord, write the letter names showing the 2 INVERSIONS of the chord.

ROOT POSITION | **INVERSIONS**

L.H. 5 3 1 R.H. 1 2 4 | L.H. 5 3 1 R.H. 1 2 5 | L.H. 5 2 1 R.H. 1 3 5

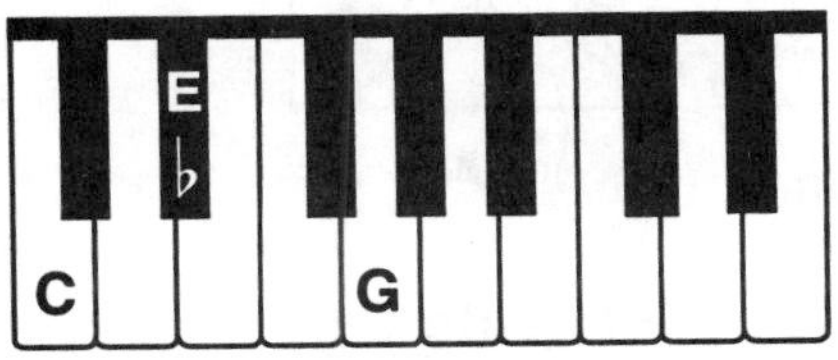

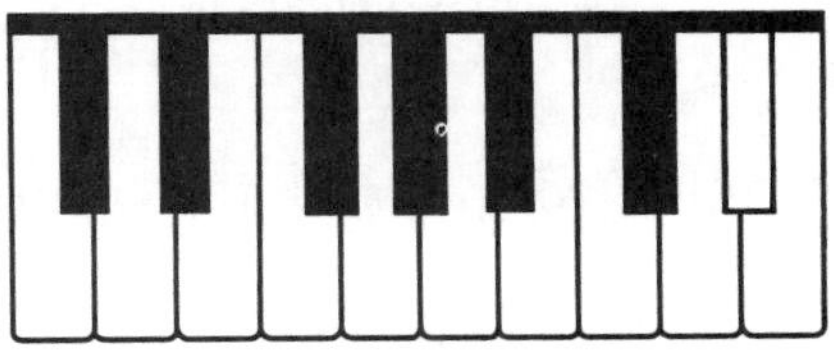

C E♭ G

i C MINOR (tonic)

L.H. 5 3 1 R.H. 1 3 5 | L.H. 5 3 1 R.H. 1 2 5 | L.H. 5 2 1 R.H. 1 3 5

F A♭ C

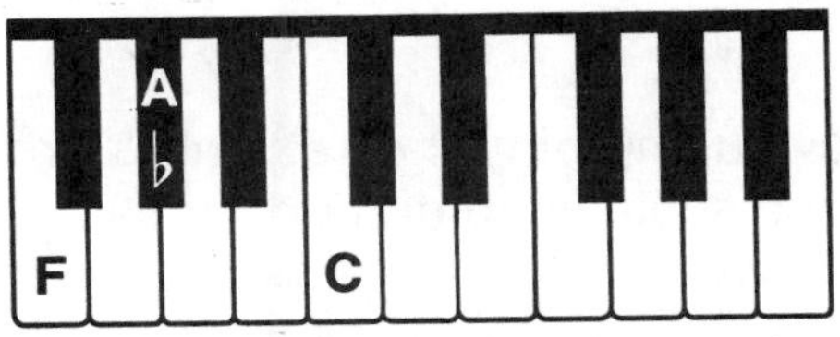

iv F MINOR (subdominant)

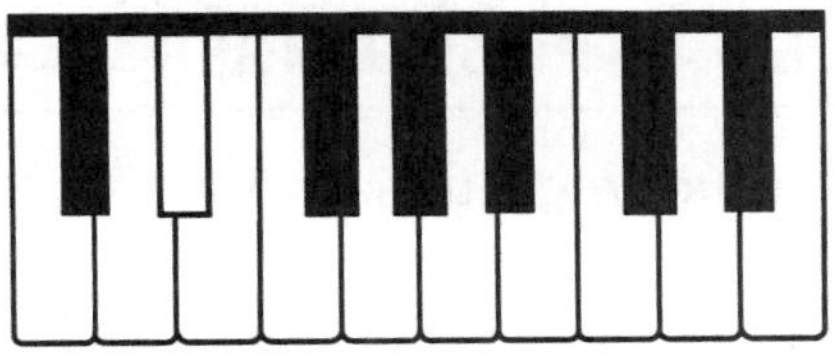

L.H. 5 3 1 R.H. 1 2 5 | L.H. 5 2 1 R.H. 1 2 4 | L.H. 4 3 1 R.H. 1 2 4

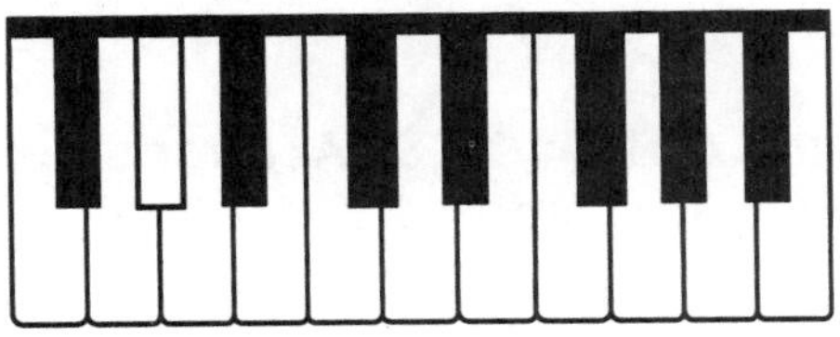

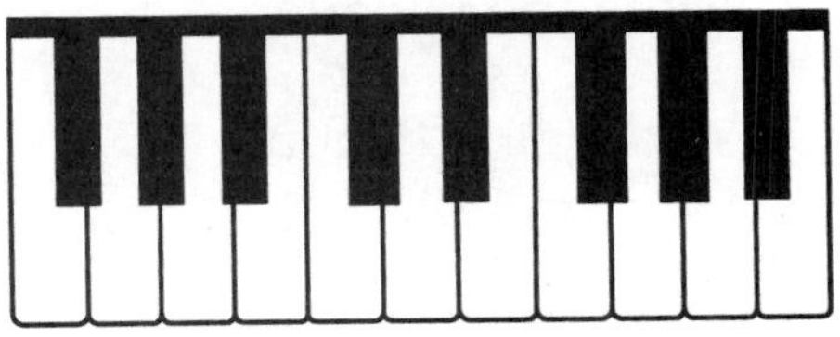

G B F

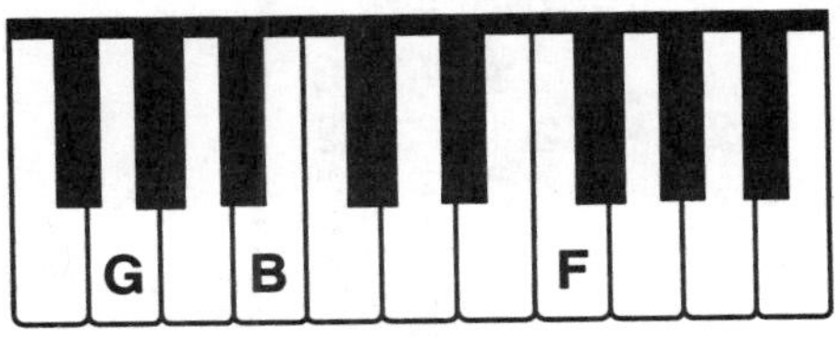

V7 (dominant 7th, 5th omitted)

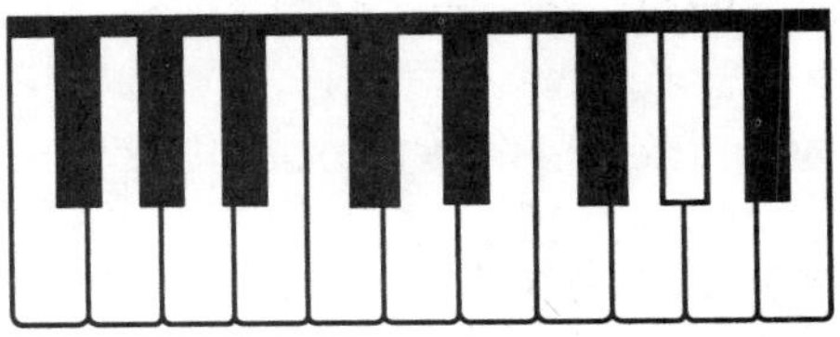

3. Play each chord shown on the above keyboards in any convenient place on your piano, first with L.H., then with R.H. Use the fingering shown above each keyboard.

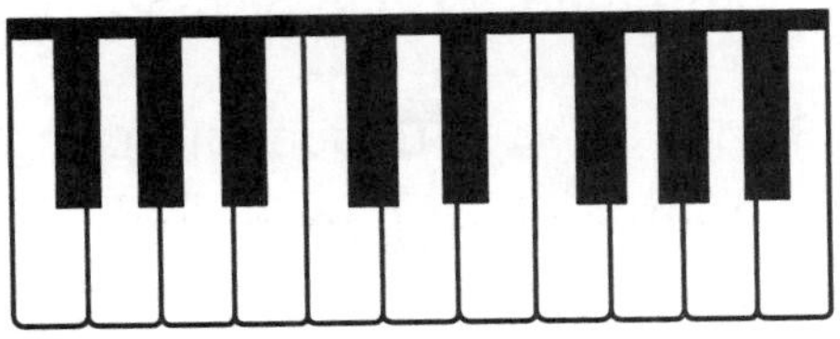

Assign with page 56.

The A♭ Major Scale

1. Write the letter names of the notes of the A♭ MAJOR SCALE, from *left to right,* on the keyboard below. Be sure the WHOLE STEPS & HALF STEPS are correct!

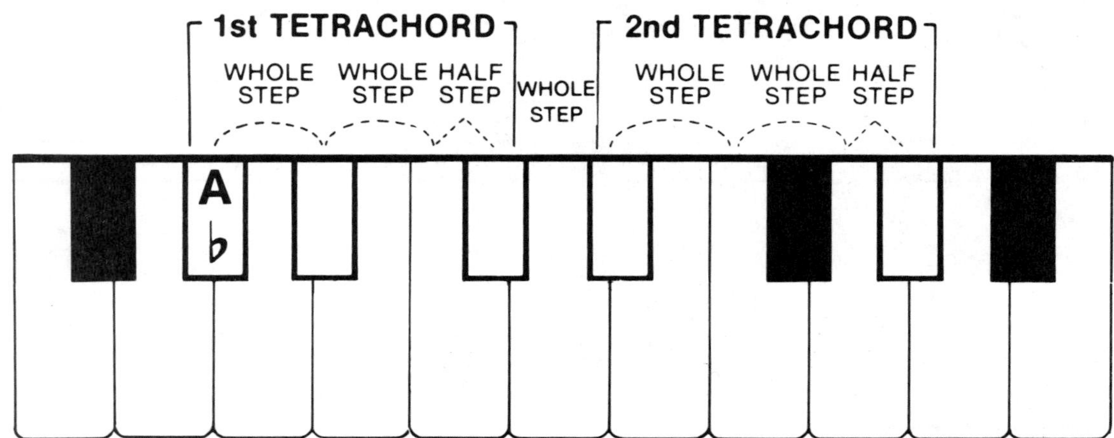

2. Check to be sure that you named the notes in the order of the musical alphabet. If you did, all the black keys will be named as *flats,* not *sharps!*

3. Complete the tetrachord beginning on A♭. Write one note over each finger number.

4. Complete the tetrachord beginning on E♭. Write one note over each finger number.

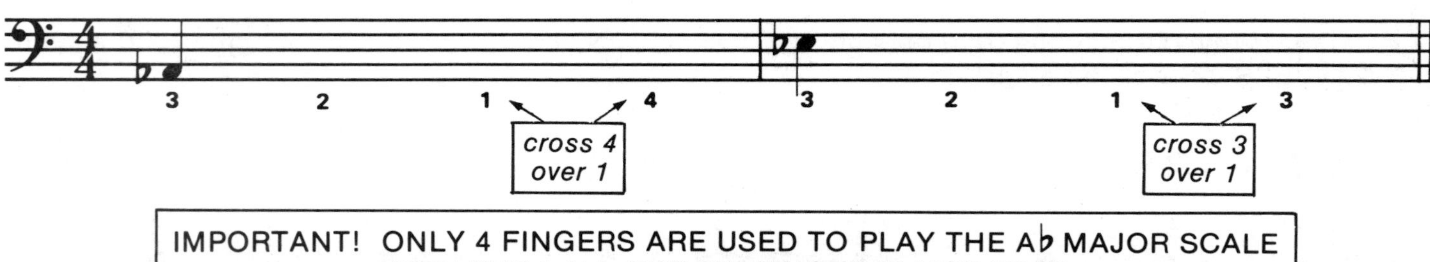

IMPORTANT! ONLY 4 FINGERS ARE USED TO PLAY THE A♭ MAJOR SCALE WITH THE L.H.! THE 5th FINGER IS NOT USED.

Beginning with L.H. 3, the scale is fingered in groups of 3 2 1 - 4 3 2 1; end on 3.

5. Write the fingering UNDER each note of the following L.H. scale.

6. Play with L.H.

With the R.H., it is possible to play the A♭ MAJOR SCALE for one octave using only the 1st, 2nd & 3rd fingers. Begin on 2, using the fingers in this order: 2 3 - 1 2 3 - 1 2 3. If the scale is continued for two or more octaves, it should be fingered: 3 4 - 1 2 3 - 1 2 3, so the second octave begins on the same finger used to end the first octave.

7. Write the fingering OVER each note of the following R.H. scale. Write the fingering required for continuing for two or more octaves in parentheses.

Ascending fingers: 2 (3) 3 (4) - 1 2 3 - 1 2 3 Descending fingers: 3 2 1 - 3 2 1 - 3 (4) 2 (3)

8. Play with R.H. several times. Try both sets of fingerings.

Assign with pages 56–59.

The Primary Chords in A♭ Major

KEY OF A♭ MAJOR
Key signature: 4 flats (B♭, E♭, A♭, & D♭)

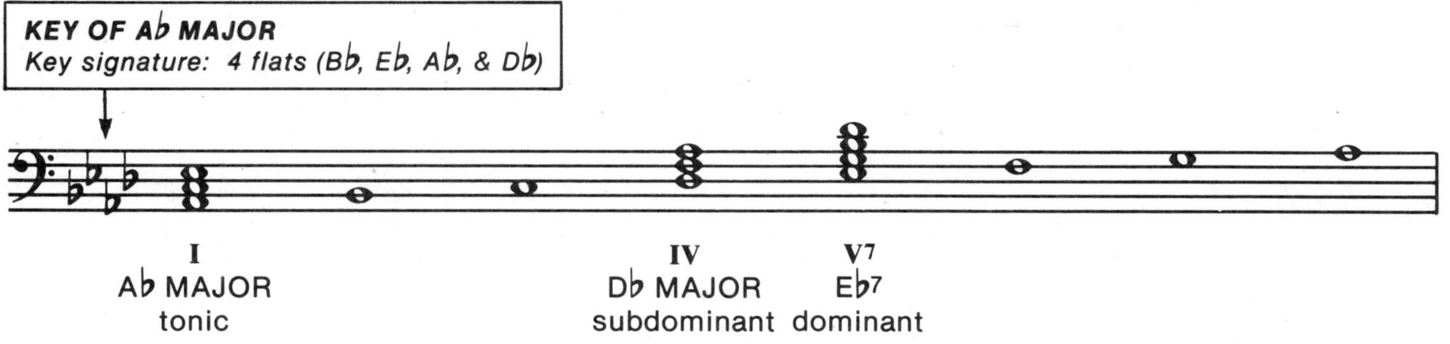

The following positions are often used for smooth progressions:

1. Add the A♭ MAJOR key signature to each staff below.
2. Write the PRIMARY CHORDS in A♭ MAJOR, using the above positions.

3. Write the ROMAN NUMERALS (**I, IV, V7**) in the boxes below.
4. Play.

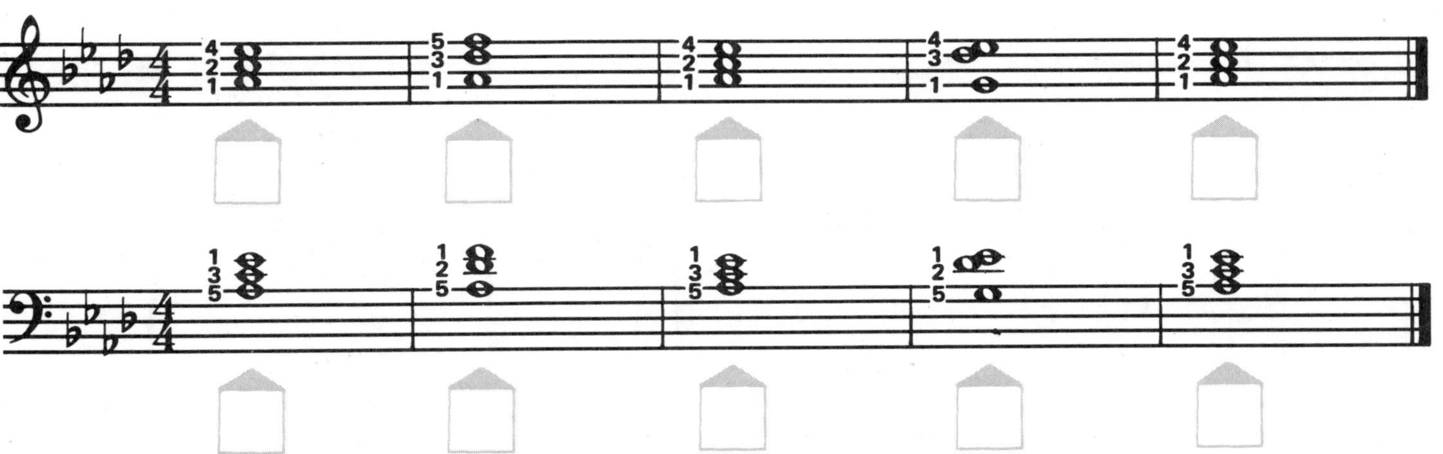

Assign with page 60.

The Primary Chords in A♭ Major—All Positions

1. In the blank measures after each ROOT POSITION chord, write the 2 INVERSIONS of the chord.

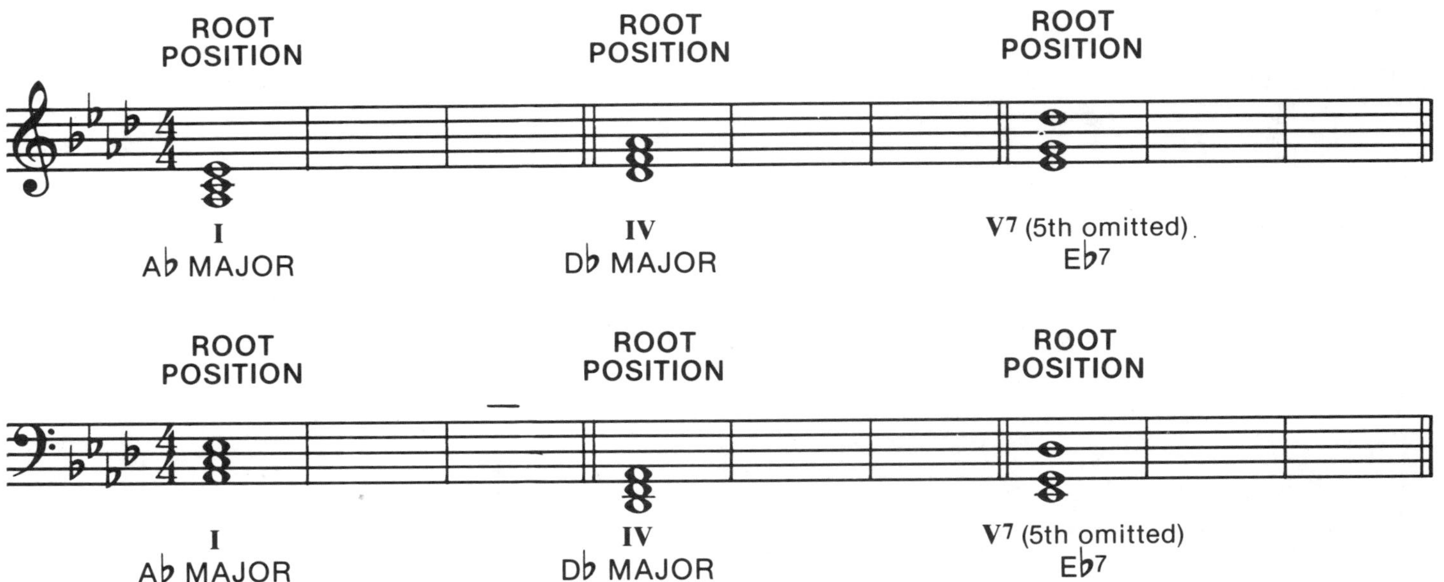

2. On the 2 keyboards to the right of each ROOT POSITION chord, write the letter names showing the 2 inversions of the chord.

ROOT POSITION — **INVERSIONS**

L.H. 5 3 1 R.H. 1 2 4 — A♭ C E♭ — L.H. 5 3 1 R.H. 1 2 5 — L.H. 5 2 1 R.H. 1 3 5

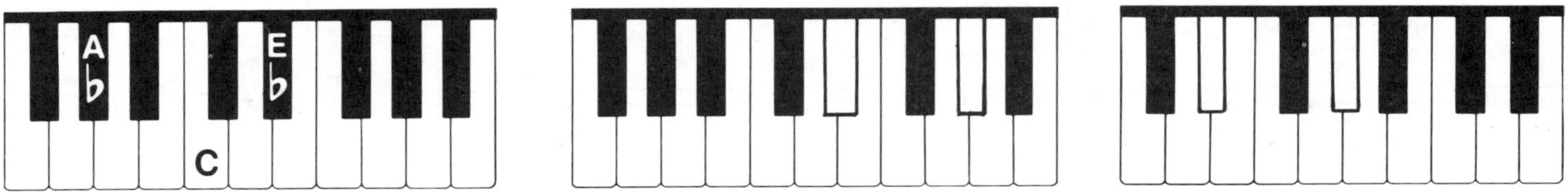

I A♭ MAJOR (tonic)

L.H. 5 3 1 R.H. 1 2 4 — D♭ F A♭ — L.H. 5 3 1 R.H. 1 2 5 — L.H. 5 2 1 R.H. 1 3 5

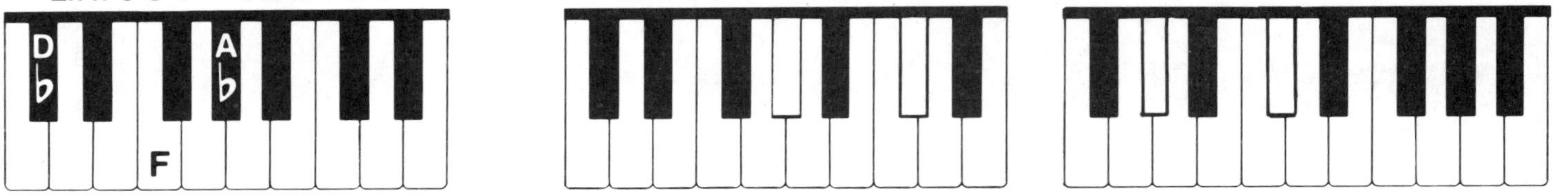

IV D♭ MAJOR (subdominant)

L.H. 5 3 1 R.H. 1 2 5 — E♭ G D♭ — L.H. 5 2 1 R.H. 1 4 5 — L.H. 4 3 1 R.H. 1 2 4

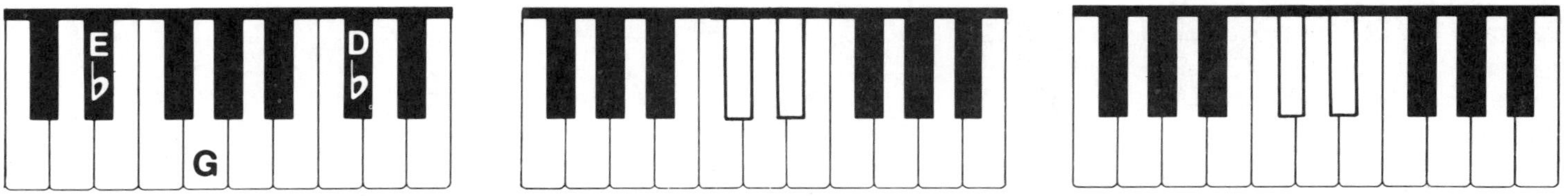

V7 E♭7 (dominant 7th, 5th omitted)

3. Play each chord shown on the above keyboards in any convenient place on your piano, first with L.H., then with R.H. Use the fingering shown above each keyboard.

Assign anytime after page 62.

Reviewing: Ornaments

ORNAMENTS are decorative notes added to melodies to make them more interesting and expressive.

Among the most important ornaments are (1) the **LONG APPOGGIATURA,** (2) the **SHORT APPOGGIATURA,** (3) the **MORDENT,** and (4) the **TRILL.**

The Long Appoggiatura

The LONG APPOGGIATURA is usually written as a small EIGHTH NOTE: ♪
The small note is played ON THE BEAT of the following LARGE NOTE, and borrows its time from the large note.

- If the large note is a whole, half, or quarter note, the small note gets HALF of its value.
- If the large note is a dotted note, the small note gets TWO-THIRDS of its value.

Matching Puzzle

Draw lines connecting the dots on the matching boxes.

Score 20 for each pair.

Perfect score equals 100.

YOUR SCORE: ____________

The Short Appoggiatura

The SHORT APPOGGIATURA is written as a small EIGHTH note with a CROSS-STROKE:
It is played VERY QUICKLY, almost together with the following large note.

Write an **S** in the box below each SHORT appoggiatura,
and an **L** in the box below each LONG appoggiatura.

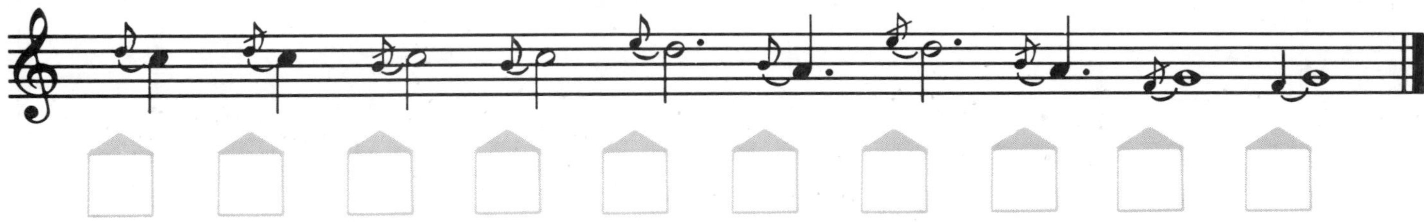

Score 10 for each correct answer. Perfect score = 100. YOUR SCORE: ________

The Mordent

Assign anytime after page 62.

- The MORDENT is indicated by this sign: 𝆖
- Rapidly play: written note, note below written note, then written note again.

may be played:
or:
or:

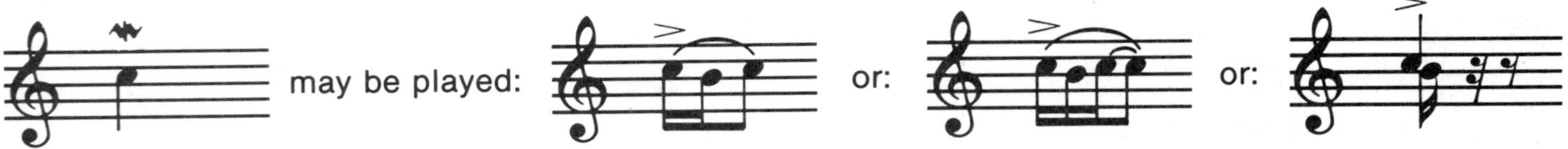

Waltz with Mordents

1. In the measure above each mordent sign, write out the mordent in full, using one of the rhythms shown above. Be sure the first note is the same as the note that appears under the sign.
2. Play.

KEY OF D MAJOR
Key Signature: 2 sharps (F♯ and C♯)

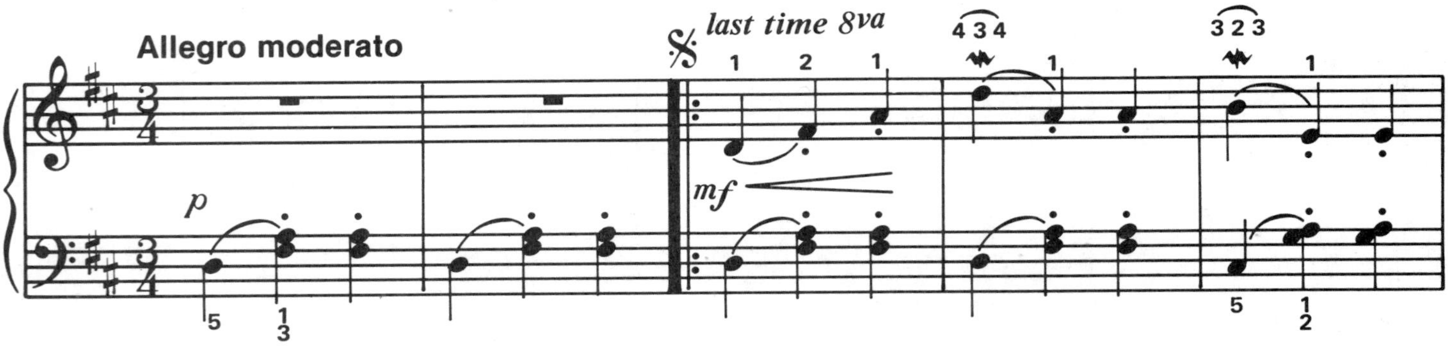
Allegro moderato
last time 8va
p
mf

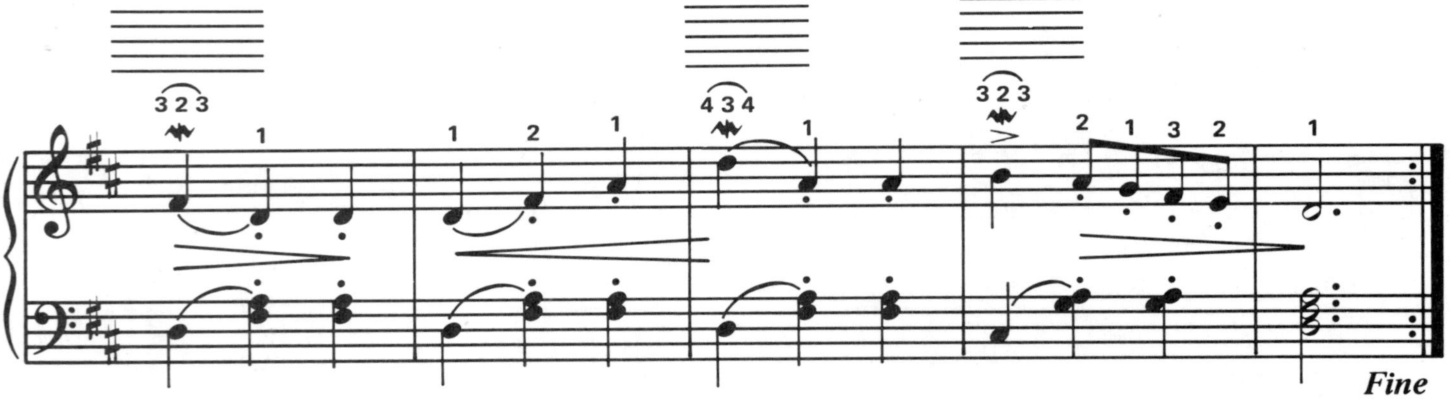
Fine

KEY OF B MINOR
Relative of D MAJOR

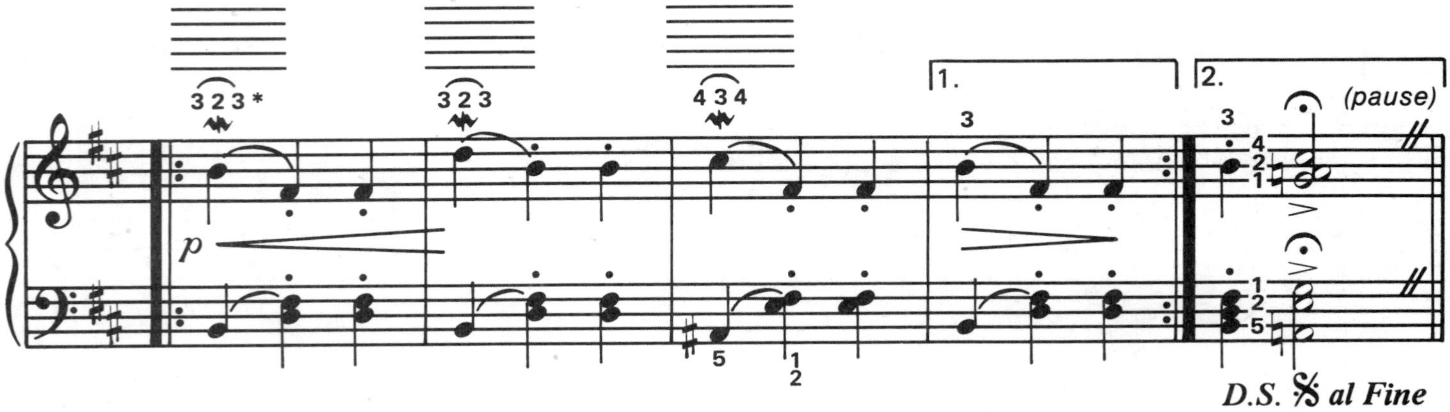
1.
2.
(pause)
p
D.S. 𝄋 al Fine

*For the lower tone of this mordent, use the raised 7th tone of the B minor scale (A♯).

The Trill

The **TRILL** is a rapid alternation of the written note with the note above it.
In some pieces, the trill is written out in notes.
In others, a TRILL SIGN is used.

The most commonly used signs for the trill are: *tr* and *tr*~~~~~~~~

In music of the 17th and 18th centuries, and most music of the early 19th century, the trill begins on the note ABOVE the written note. In later music the trill begins on the WRITTEN note. In *Alfred's Basic Piano Library,* you will always be shown how each trill should be played.

Trills do not always need to have an EXACT number of notes. They may be played faster than the above notes indicate, with additional alternations of the two notes, but they must fit into the time value of the note.

Trills starting on the UPPER note are expressive and brilliant. They are like rapidly repeated UPPER APPOGGIATURAS, and have a similar effect on the melody.

Trills starting on the WRITTEN note are simply decorative, since they do not affect the melody.

Mozart's Trill Exercise

This valuable exercise was handed down to us by one of Mozart's most famous pupils, J. N. Hummel. If you practice it daily you will be able to trill with all combinations of fingers with either hand!

Practice the entire exercise slowly at first. Gradually increase speed.

Assign anytime after page 62.

This piece is part of a larger composition for wind instruments, strings and drums. It is typical of the festive music played in the French courts in the early 1700's. It has become a familiar favorite because of its use as the theme for the popular television series, *Masterpiece Theatre.*

RONDEAU

Jean Joseph Mouret (1682–1753)
Transcribed by P.M.L.

Andante

tr
2nd time ritardando
Fine
mf
D.C. al Fine

Assign anytime after page 62.

Completing the Circle of 5ths:

The Flat Key Signatures

Beginning with C and moving downward in 5ths COUNTER-CLOCKWISE, the order of keys around the circle is

C F B♭ E♭ A♭ D♭ G♭ C♭

Each key has one more FLAT than the previous one, as you move around the circle.

The key of C MAJOR has NO FLATS.

The key of F MAJOR has 1 FLAT (B♭).

The key of B♭ MAJOR has 2 FLATS (B♭ & E♭), etc., continuing around the circle until all the notes are flat.

The key of C♭ MAJOR has 7 FLATS: B♭, E♭, A♭, D♭, G♭, C♭ & F♭.

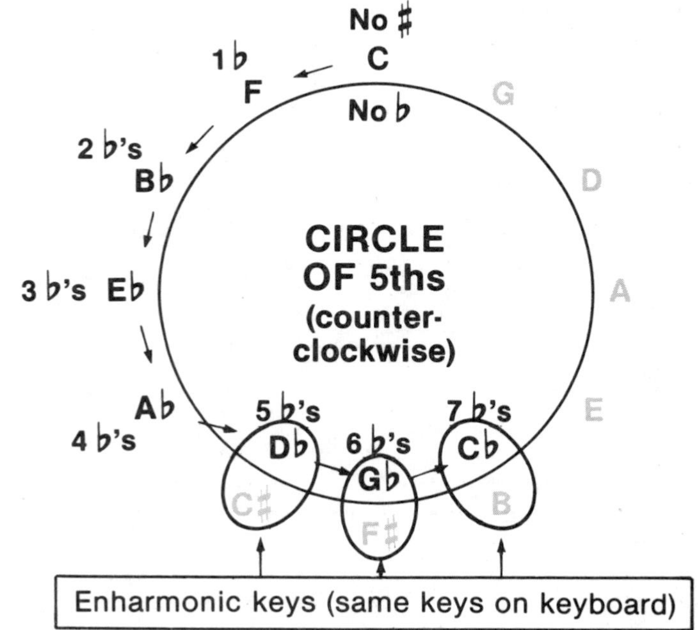

1. Copy the flats of each key signature in the blank measure following it.

IMPORTANT!!

Notice that the flats in the key signatures occur in the order of the letters (moving counter-clockwise) around the Circle of 5ths, beginning with B♭.

B♭ E♭ A♭ D♭ G♭ C♭ F♭